Kitty Kapers

Dozens and Dozens of Indoor and Outdoor Activities for You and Your Feline Friend—Tricks and Games, Arts and Crafts, Stories and Songs, and Much More!

Martha Bayless

TEN SPEED PRESS
Berkeley / Toronto

This book has benefited from the expertise of many, among them
Mabel Armstrong, Aletta and Sasha Biersack, Dave Bischoff, John Burridge, Ruth Clark,
Lee Kirk, Vickie Nelson, Steve Shurtleff, Bill Sullivan, and Leslie What. It could not have
existed without the generous guidance of Erin Slonaker. And, most of all, the author is
grateful for the advice of the real experts: Teemer, Beastie, Pouncer, and Grizzle.

A Kirsty Melville Book

Ten Speed Press
P.O. Box 7123
Berkeley, California 94707
www.tenspeed.com

Distributed in Canada by Ten Speed Press Canada.

Design by Susan Van Horn
Illustrations by Alexander Stadler

A Quirk Book
www.quirkproductions.com

Library of Congress Cataloging-in-Publication Data
Bayless, Martha, 1958-
Kitty kapers : dozens and dozens of indoor and outdoor activities for you and your feline friend:
tricks and games, arts and crafts, stories and songs, and much more! / Martha Bayless.
p. cm.
ISBN 1-58008-438-9 (alk. paper)
1. Cats—Exercise. 2. Cats—Equipment and supplies. 3. Handicraft. I. Title.
SF446.7.B38 2002
636.8'089371—dc21
2002020194

First printing, 2002
Printed in Singapore by Tien Wah

1 2 3 4 5 6 7 8 9 10-04 03 02

Contents

CONTENTS

Introduction

If you have a cat (or cats—like potato chips, it's hard to have just one), you already know about lazy naps, frisky romps, and the sheer sensual enjoyment of a spot in the sun. This book is to remind you of all those simple joys and to suggest advanced great big fun you can have with your kitty friends. You can cultivate catnip together, cook Mackerel Snackerels, wiggle string, read (or write) great kitty literature, construct Kitty Catstles, or even create a Web site about your cat. There's no end to the possibilities! Our purring kitty helpers, Fred and Ginger, are standing by to demonstrate games, quizzes, and treats. Let this book be a *catalyst* for all kinds of furry feline fun!

CHAPTER ONE

Big Game Playing

All cats are big game hunters—not only in the wilds of the backyard, but in the territory of the indoors, where wild string, paper bags, and catnip mice roam. Here are some of the most popular big games to play with kitty, as well as the big games that kitty plays with you. All you need are a few simple items such as socks, sheets, and string. There's also fun to be had in kitty tricks, from jumping through a hoop to purring by telepathy. Fred and Ginger have tested the following games thoroughly for cat-pleasability. As they say in New Orleans, *Laissez les bons temps ronronner!* *

* Let the good times purr!

3

Games to Play with Kitty

The Bag Game

A grocery bag is to most cats what a garbage can is to a black bear: something they must, must, must get inside. Once inside, the fun begins.

WHAT YOU'LL NEED:

- one large paper grocery bag

WHAT YOU'LL DO:

Lay the bag on its side on the floor. Once Ginger's in the bag, poke and tap at the bag's closed end for lots of pouncing fun. She'll be especially intrigued if you tickle the bag, then pause . . . pause . . . pause . . . tickle again. That pause has been known to drive cats certifiably crazy with anticipation.

Another variant: toss a toy mouse into the bag. If you have two cats, one can do the inner pouncing, one the outer. Or you can cut a cat-sized or paw-sized hole in the

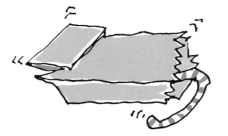

bag for greater intrigue. This can go on until, well, the cat's out of the bag.

The Hand-in-the-Sock Game

WHAT YOU'LL NEED:

- **one big thick sock**

WHAT YOU'LL DO:

Put your hand in the sock and pretend it's a sock puppet on the prowl, like Shari Lewis's Lamb Chop on steroids. Then the Sock Creature can sneak up on kitty, walking on tiptoe or scrunching like an inchworm. Once Fred has a good grip on the Sock Creature, the Creature can flail mightily, and you'll be protected from injury—hopefully—by sock armor. (Warning: Play gently. If Fred runs away, you've been playing too hard. If you're bleeding, Fred's been playing too hard.) If sock armor still leaves you vulnerable, try putting your hand in an oven mitt instead. Apart from this, the only downside of this game is that Fred may get the idea that any sock, even a sock still on a human foot, is game for an attack. On the upside, this could be a way to get rid of unwanted guests: "Auntie Beulah and Uncle Grumpus! What a surprise! Do take off your shoes and make yourselves at home! Oh . . . oh dear . . . bad Fred! Well, cats will be cats—you say you're leaving already?"

The Changing-the-Sheets Game

WHAT YOU'LL NEED:

- one bed
- one fresh pair of sheets

WHAT YOU'LL DO:

Spreading out sheets on a bed is like waving a red cape in front of a bull. Many cats will bound aboard the mattress, ready to charge. When the sheet comes down over them, they'll be transformed into Anonymous Bumps underneath. With your hand, make mouselike rustlings and scurryings on top of the sheet, and watch the Bump pounce. This can go on for many, many hours. If you lift up the sheet, however, you'll be faced with a very disappointed kitty whose expression will say, "But how did you know it was me under here?"

The Laser Pointer Game

WHAT YOU'LL NEED:

- one laser pointer

WHAT YOU'LL DO:

Be one of the thousand points of light! Turn on the laser pointer and aim the dot of light at the floor, where kitty will try to seize and eat it. The first time Fred encounters the point of light, he'll try to put his paw on it, and then, of course, the dot of light will end up on top of his paw. So he'll put his other paw on that. And that stubborn dot of light will stay on top of his paw. So he'll take the first paw out from under the second . . . Like a mouse, it's a renewable source of energetic fun, but much healthier for the local fauna. Warning: Don't aim the pointer at anyone's eyes. For traditionalists, a flashlight will also work, although you'll have to turn out the lights before Fred will respond.

Stringing Them Along

WHAT YOU'LL NEED:

- a string long enough to reach from your hand to the floor

For best results, tie a knot in kitty's end of the string, then wriggle the string until Ginger is totally pooped. Hints: She'll like it better if the string snakes along the ground instead of being dangled in the air. (If you want to dangle it in the air, tie a mouselike object or, better yet, a wad of crinkly cellophane on the end for better grabbing fun.) She'll like it best if you pull the string around a corner, and she won't pounce until the string has just disappeared—the better to keep the string from seeing her, my dear!

For a variant, try using knitting yarn, which has the advantage of being stretchy. You can amuse Ginger while making a baby blanket for Cousin Abigail! Call this game Knit One, Purr Too.

Games Kitty Plays with You

The Midnight Ricochet

WHAT KITTY NEEDS:

• **one late night**

You are getting sleepy, very sleepy . . . and Fred is getting frisky, very frisky. Soon mere balls of string won't do it. Scientific studies have shown that cats actually morph into 70 percent vulcanized rubber after 11:30 P.M., which is why they're able to bounce from one side of the house to the other with such energy late at night. It's a little-known fact that wild cats do it too. Those jungle earthquakes you see in B movies? Panthers, rocketing through the Amazon. The only possible response is to grab a bed and sit tight until the ruckus passes.

The Furball Express

* **everything kitty needs here is self-generated, although the whole game is more fun if played on a carpet**

There's actually a symbol in the International Phonetic Alphabet for the sound kitty makes when bringing up a furball: /X/. This is the same in every language, which shows that the Furball Express goes back to the dawn of time, when humans hadn't even thought up how to say "Ew! Gross!" in Indo-European. The Furball Express consists of repeated enunciations of this sound, like cheers at a football game, followed by a tangible souvenir that the game has been completed. The outdoor variant is entitled Eat Grass and Puke.

The Blood Sacrifice Game
(I Brought You This Because I Love You)

WHAT KITTY NEEDS:

- **a small catchable critter**

WHAT KITTY DOES:

Ginger shows her devotion to you by bringing you a small delicacy from your own yard. Sacrifices to the Higher Power go back to the Old Testament, after all, and cats are traditionalists. True, in the Old Testament the receptacle for the sacrifice was more majestic than a mere doormat, and the sacrifice typically was more than three inches in length, but never mind the lack of grandeur—isn't it flattering just to be considered a Higher Power? Even if the Higher Power is the one who has to clean off the doormat?

The advanced version (entitled "I've Hidden Your Present") has all the fun of the Blood Sacrifice Game with all the drama of Hide and Seek. Your nose tells you the game is afoot, but it's up to you to locate the prize. Oh, the fun Ginger has watching you search the house!

Teaching an Old Cat New Tricks

Contrary to what Fred and Ginger may claim, it is indeed possible to teach them to respond to your commands—or should we call them "requests"? Of course, for these tricks you don't have to have an old cat—even a young cat will do.

The main way in which cats differ from dogs is that, much as they love you, they won't learn tricks merely to please you. ("We roll on our backs, we purr, we accept rubs," says Ginger. "That's not pleasing enough?") Edible treats are necessary for use as motivators. The best treats are those that your cat already loves. Pick the treat your cat loves best and give it to your cat only during training sessions for the duration of the training period.

For the greatest success, train your cat just before mealtime, with no distractions around. Keep training sessions very short—if Ginger loses interest, you've lost the battle. The training period, which lasts until your cat has been trained, can last for as little as a few weeks, but may go on for years. Be patient. Important points to remember are:

Be consistent. Ask for the same behavior the same way each time.

Show her what you want. Your cat can't read your mind: you may have to show her what's wanted in small steps over a period of some days. Remain patient, and never, ever, scold her for not understanding.

Be grateful for small successes. There's a reason a cat isn't a dog. Ginger may never pick up a ball in her mouth, dash along the riverbank, cross the river on a tree trunk, run through the woods, jump over a pasture fence, open the front gate

11

with her paws, drop the ball, and bark for attention, thereby letting little Timmy's mother know that he was hurt playing catch down at the Greenfields' farm. But then, Lassie can't even purr. If Ginger comes when called and does a few other simple tricks, that's more than most of the cats in town, and you both are entitled to hold your heads up high.

Which tricks to choose? Cats, like dogs, will only do things on command that they were inclined to do anyway: you don't so much affect *what* they do as *when* they do it. So look out for things that your cat already does that you might like to encourage. If Ginger carries a toy mouse or a wad of scrunched-up paper around in her mouth, you may be able to teach her to fetch. If Fred already has the hang of opening drawers, you may be able to teach him to open drawers on command. If Ginger jumps onto her cat

tree in a single bound, it's likely you can teach her to do it when you say "Jump!" And if Fred likes to do nothing other than lie around in the sun—well, "Lie down!" has always been a favorite command.

Here are a few very simple commands to teach your cat, and then, for the trick-impaired, a few Incredibly Simple Tricks Your Cat Can Do Every Time.

Come. Your cat probably already comes when you walk into the kitchen at dinnertime. Now all you need to do is add the words "Here, Ginger!" or "Come, Ginger!" to the ritual. (Allowing for adjustments, of course, if your cat's name is not Ginger!) Say the command every time, produce food soon thereafter, and in a short while she'll come when you say the command even if you're not in the kitchen or it's not dinnertime. To reinforce the behavior, give her a kitty treat from time to time when she answers your call. (If, however, you put her in the cat car-rier for a trip to the vet every time she answers your call, she may unlearn the behavior very quickly.)

Through the Hoop. This is a trick for energetic cats. Get a hoop your cat can step through easily: a large embroidery hoop will do. The first time, put the hoop between your cat and a dish with a kitty treat in it so she steps through the hoop on the way to the treat. As you position the hoop, say, "Hoop, Ginger." Repeat this for a few days, each time saying "Hoop, Ginger" as you proffer the hoop with the treat on the other side of it. Then just put the hoop in position, say "Hoop, Ginger," and lay the treat on the floor for her to step through the hoop and get. Graduate to offering her the treat from your hand as you say, "Hoop, Ginger," and she steps through the hoop. Take this in slow, gradual stages until you can say, "Hoop, Ginger," and she understands that stepping through the hoop means that a treat will be produced. If she's quite energetic and eager, you can then move on to raising the hoop a bit. Ginger says, "Don't forget that treat!" Even if you get to the point where she'll pop through the hoop at a moment's notice, give her a reward treat from time to time.

Stand Up. Some cats get up on their hind legs to beg or to inspect things they can't see otherwise; the more your cat is a natu-ral hind-leg-stander, the easier it will be to train him to do this on command.

Palm one of your cat's favorite treats, let him know it's in your palm, and raise your hand to a level where he can get it only by standing. Say, "Stand, Fred!" When he stands to get the treat, give it to him with great praise. Repeat once for reinforcement, but if you do it too many times in a row he'll lose interest, so hold off until the next day. Within a week he should understand that "Stand, Fred!" and the palming of the kitty treat will mean he'll get the treat if he stands.

Purr. If your cat's a willing purrer, you can actually teach her to purr by giving her a "command" from afar. Every time you pat her enough to start her purring, make a small noise that can be associated with the patting session. For those who don't mind being labeled "too, too precious" by onlookers, repeated kissy noises work very well. If you make the kissy noises consistently during patting-and-purring sessions, eventually you will be able to jump-start purring without actually touching your cat. Wait until she's curled up in a comfy position, look down at her and achieve eye contact, and make the kissy noise at her. A big rumble of a purr will start up. Of course, you will have to reward this responsiveness with lots of patting!

Incredibly Simple Tricks Your Cat Can Do Every Time

So Fred's one of those stubborn cats who thinks eating out of the food dish is all a cat should have to accomplish? Put those convictions to good use with these simple commands Fred's guaranteed to obey!

Meow on Command. This command works like a charm at dinnertime. Wait until Fred is haunting the kitchen waiting for his canned-catfood dinner. Take out the can opener. Rattle the food dish. Set the can of catfood on the counter. Command "Say meow, Fred!" Open and close the can opener and rattle the food dish some more. Fred's meowing by now, right? See what a cooperative cat he is?

Purr (by telepathy). Pat Fred extensively. Massage his back, pat his tummy, stroke underneath his chin. Wait until he's all sprawled out, half rolled over, in abject kitty delight. Command, "Purr, Fred!" But wait! Fred was already purring, wasn't he? He read your mind telepathically and obeyed your command even before you made it aloud! If that's not obedience, what is?

Stay. Wait until Fred is all curled up and deeply asleep. Command (softly), "Stay, Fred!" Who said Fred wouldn't follow orders?

Stay (from a distance). Observe that Fred is sleeping in a distant part of the house. Go to the living room. Say, in a quiet, non-cat-disturbing tone, "Stay where you are, Fred!" Even from a great distance, Fred will obey!

For an extra test of Fred's mettle, prepare a dish of ice cream. Again, make sure that Fred is asleep in a distant part of the house. (For best results, do not do this at Fred's dinnertime or use any dishes Fred might associate with his own food.) Settle in a recliner with the ice cream and command, "Fred, stay where you are until I eat this entire bowl of ice cream!" This tests Fred's obedience over a period of time. You may wish to practice this trick often to be sure Fred's ability to sleep through the whole bowl of ice cream stays sharp.

Kitty Characteristics

To paraphrase George Orwell, all kitties are equal, but some are more equal than others. To paraphrase Garrison Keillor, they're all above average! You can tell a great deal about your cat by looking at his language, dialect, behavior—and, of course, past eight lives. After all, he spends a great deal of time watching your every move (toward the refrigerator) and musing on your every remark (and you thought he was just sleeping!). Now you can analyze him in return. "Where would you like me to lie, Dr. Freud?" asks Fred. "On the couch? I thought you'd never ask!"

Kitty Kommunication

Kitty Kommunication goes far beyond meowing, as anyone who's experienced tail-lashing cat disapproval will recognize. Here's a guide to the ways in which Ginger communicates with the world, with the meaning of each expression as interpreted by top experts.

"Meow": "I have something to say. You guess. No, I am not going to be more specific about it."

"MEOW, MEOW": "Something is very wrong! Something is very wrong! Dish out the catfood / Tell me where you are / Open the door / Stop ignoring me—right now!"

"M'w": "Hey, thanks."

"Purrrr": "Mmm. Do that some more."

"Purrup!": "Hiya!"

Tail high in air: "Oh boy, life is good."

Tail trailing along behind: "Ho hum. Just walking around looking for something to do. No need to feel guilty about how dull your household is. My expectations were low."

Rolling over onto back: "Hee hee. You can pet my belly if you like."

Trying to roll onto side of face: "Catnip—the best. I'll just put some in my ear here for safekeeping."

Ears back: "I am displeased."

Ears way back: "I should mention that my displeasure is increasing."

Ears flat back against head: "In fact, I am going to shred someone's arm (or someone's doggy friend) within seconds if someone doesn't back off."

Tail-thumping: "You didn't notice my ears? Then check out the tail. I'm angry and I mean what I say, bud."

"Grrrr": "I sharpen my claws daily, and if you come one millimeter closer I'll give you a close-up of my manicure."

"Hissss!": "You are a dog, an unfriendly cat, or the vet, and I don't care which, because I recognize you as the spawn of Satan."

"MOW!": "Hey, big oaf! Watch where you're stepping!"

As far as language goes, cats are much like the French: they speak their own tongue with flair, but they have nothing but polite disdain for foreigners like you who try to imitate them. So when you say "Meow!" to Fred, he may look at you with a deliberately unreadable expression, but he's actually thinking, "Oh, what an accent! If she can't pull off the feline *mm*, poor thing, she shouldn't even try."

There are, however, a few tricks to make communicating with cats easier:

- ▶ When meeting cats for the first time, crouch or at least sit down. This keeps you from being a towering hulk and makes you more normal-sized, and less intimidating, in their eyes.

- ▶ Many cats will come to you if you hold out one hand and rub your thumb and index finger together. There is something hypnotic in this gesture.

- ▶ When greeting a cat you're just meeting, or haven't seen for a while, hold out your index finger and let him sniff it. Cats sniff each other's noses on meeting, and the tip of your index finger is just the size of a cat nose. It's only polite to offer it, like offering a hand to shake when meeting a person, and the cat will acknowledge your politeness. If you've already talked or interacted, however, he'll be less interested (after all, you don't shake hands once a conversation has already started).

- ▶ To indicate that your lap is ready for cat occupation, pat your lap audibly while a cat is looking your way. This is an invitation but not a command, so don't be put out if she walks on by.

- ▶ The ultimate sign of happy symbiosis with your cat: when you can start her purring merely by looking at her from afar.

The Kitty Dialect Test

Sure, all cats speak the same language, but not always with the same accent. Is your kitty a country bumpkin, a suave cat-about-town, or an uptown puss? Test your cat's dialect and find out!

1. **Your cat says:**

    a) mew.

    b) meow.

    c) MROWW!

2. **When you're slow getting kitty's dinner ready, your cat will say:**

    a) mew.

    b) meow, meow, meow, meow, meow!

    c) ROWWWWWWR!

    ROWWWWWWR!

    ROWWWWWWR!

3. **Your cat's purr sounds like:**

    a) the quietest, gentlest rumble.

    b) an outboard motor.

    c) a chainsaw.

4. **When meeting strange cats, your cat will say something like:**

    a) [dignified silence]

    b) mrrrrow?

    c) grrrrr. Hssssss!

5. **When you open a door for your cat, he will:**

a) look up at you and purr before going through.

b) say "thank you" ("mrow" or "mew") loudly.

c) stride through with the silence of satisfied entitlement.

Count up the number of a's, b's, and c's.

Mostly a's: The Cat-About-Town Charmer (otherwise known as "Cat. James Cat."). Your cat comes from dignified city parents who most likely sent their little one to Kitten Charm School. He or she washes paws after every meal (and behind the ears), says "please" and "thank you," and can handle situations demanding the most complicated etiquette. The perfect companion for a night at the opera or a diplomatic dinner.

Mostly b's: The Enthusiast. What your cat lacks in refinement, he or she makes up for in warmth of emotion, good-heartedness, and eagerness for treats. Your cat most likely grew up in the suburbs, in a split-level house, and started college but dropped out because he overdid it on the tuna one term, then got a job supervising mice removal at the local warehouse. He still prefers mouse-watching to the more contemplative arts, and a good piece of yarn can keep him fascinated for hours.

Mostly c's: The Diamond in the Rough. Your cat may have seen the inside of a shelter, but despite having been behind bars, he or she has a heart of pure gold and the rough-hewn manners of a true original. Whether stalking toy mice by day or patrolling the fences by night, this seen-it-all, done-it-all feline will speak his mind, and to heck with grammar!

The Kitty Personality Test

Want a professional assessment of your cat's personality? Take the following test:

1. **If you put a leash on your cat, he would:**
   a) assume an extremely grumpy expression and lie down.
   b) follow you reluctantly.
   c) pull you along after him in his eagerness to go for a walk.

2. **Your cat meows:**
   a) in times of desperate extremity, such as needing to go in or out, when you're slow with the can opener, when he can't get at a bird just outside the window, and so forth.
   b) throughout the day, by way of casual commentary.
   c) when he is awakened by something or wants to warn you of something.

3. **When your cat meets people he doesn't know:**
   a) he is either standoffish or ignores them—unless they dislike cats, in which case he's all over them immediately.
   b) he stands at a distance and eyes them cagily, then may become friendly.
   c) he greets them at the door and tries to jump on them.

4. **Your cat's ideal day would be:**

   a) eat, lie around in the sun, eat more.

   b) eat, complain, bounce around, complain some more.

   c) eat, bounce around a lot, eat, bounce around some more.

5. **Your cat will obey orders:**

   a) rarely. For instance, if you're opening a can of cat food and you call his name at the same time, he might come.

   b) occasionally. He'll sometimes come when called, and he likes treats so much you suspect you might be able to train him, but you haven't bothered.

   c) almost always. He comes when called, likes to beg for treats, and is otherwise more than eager to do whatever you want done.

6. **Your cat's favorite activity:**

   a) is to lie around and be patted, although if he's feeling frisky, he might try to nip your hand every once in a while.

   b) is to lie around and be patted, although there's a very good chance he'll try to chomp your hand at some point.

   c) is to run around while you throw things for him.

Mostly a's: Your cat is certified "Normal" by the International Society for Feline Psychology. In other words, your cat's personality is characterized by affection, aloofness, excessive energy, laziness, dissatisfaction, contentment, eagerness, indecision, and a liking for kitty treats. Your cat's mottos are "If only there were something really good to eat" and "I'll just lie down here."

Mostly b's: Your cat is certified "Siamese" by the International Society for Feline Psychology. Your cat may look like a Siamese, Burmese, or other similar breed, or be jet black, but he or she will be characterized by an assertive personality, self-assurance, affection, aloofness, determination, strong verbal skills, and a liking for kitty treats. Your cat's mottos are "But I was lying on this" and "You are not following my instructions!"

Mostly c's: You have a dog. Please examine your cat again and compare with a picture of a "dog" in any standard reference work. See? Didn't we tell you? Please make a note of it.

The First Eight Lives
What Great Person Has Been Reincarnated as Your Cat?

Let's get this clear: there are no cats who were simply lowly peasants in their past lives. They were all great personages—any cat will tell you that. But which personage? That's where the Cat Reincarnation-Finder comes in.

Add up the points for each appropriate answer.

1. **Is your cat:**
   a) very timid (1 point).
   b) shy at times (2 points).
   c) easygoing (3 points).
   d) friendly and sociable (4 points).
   e) always the center of attention (5 points).

2. **If your cat played a human game, it would be:**
   a) chess, possibly even three-dimensional chess (1 point).
   b) Scrabble (2 points).
   c) poker (3 points).
   d) go fish (4 points).
   e) tiddlywinks (5 points).

3. **Does your cat:**
   a) hate all other cats (1 point).
   b) dislike most other cats (2 points).
   c) act indifferent toward other cats (3 points).
   d) like most other cats (4 points).
   e) snuggle up with another cat at a moment's notice (5 points).

4. **If your cat could hunt and catch anything it wanted, it would catch:**
   a) string (1 point).
   b) bugs (2 points).
   c) songbirds (3 points).
   d) turkey vultures (4 points).
   e) moose (5 points).

If your cat is female, in a past life she was:

6 points or less: Marie Curie

7–10 points: Queen Victoria

11–14 points: Queen Elizabeth I

15–17 points: Mata Hari

18–20 points: Cleopatra

If your cat is male, in a past life he was:

6 points or less: Albert Einstein

7–10 points: Socrates

11–14 points: William Shakespeare

15–17 points: King Henry VIII

18–20 points: Alexander the Great

But you say, they can't *all* have been Alexander the Great or Cleopatra! Tell that to Fred or Ginger! Ginger says, "I certainly was Cleopatra, and so was my mother and so were all my sisters! And the cat next door and that hussy-cat down the street! The only difference is that I am the most dignified and magnificent Cleopatra—and don't you forget it! Incidentally, did you know that Cleopatra's favorite food was tuna?"

Secret Kitty Kosmic Knowledge

Why are cats so energetic at night? While you're asleep, they're at school, learning secret kitty kosmic knowledge. What does Fred do when he disappears for the day? He's enrolled in an intensive course at Cat University. Why does Ginger sleep all day long? Catnaps are a proven form of deep philosophical thinking which will someday form part of her Ph.D. (Pheline Doctorate). Cats have kept this knowledge from us for millennia, knowing that the effort of thinking deeply leads to inertia and reduced expertise with the can opener. As a special human treat, however, Fred and Ginger have agreed to outline the most vital subjects known to cats.

Astronomy

Cats are nocturnal. They look up a great deal. Is it any wonder that the scientific study of the night sky is very important to them? When Fred is on the windowsill looking out, he's doing nothing less than performing his studies, identifying Pisces, Mus, Orion's Mouse, and the rest. Is it any wonder cats can find their way around at night? The lesson here is that gazing out of a window in apparent laziness is more praiseworthy than you might think.

Mathematics

Cats are so advanced in this subject that it's no wonder that most of us are clueless about cat mathematics. The most vital lesson we can learn from math cats: there doesn't have to be a decimal system. (Why do you think cats feel free to have more than five toes per paw? They don't need them to count with!) In fact, cat math is so advanced it has dispensed with most numbers entirely. There are only two basic concepts in cat math: zero and infinity. The more advanced mathecaticians are beginning to discard the zero as well, leaving only infinity. Notice, for instance, how many times Ginger will scratch at a door to be let in—countless times. Dogs will give up when they reach the heights their limited minds can touch. Cats, on the other hand, never stop.

The cat science of the Infinite therefore, is an important concept. Ginger suggests you begin your own study of the Infinite with dishes of tuna.

Biology

Feline enthusiasm for biology is unparalleled. Consider the evidence:

Eating. In human universities, students are considered diligent if they spend three hours a day in a biology lab, and yet Ginger puts in hours eating, thinking about eating, asking for food, and experimenting to determine the exact delineation between the delectable and the unacceptable. And then she concentrates very hard on the digestive process, which involves lying stretched out.

Snoozing. We tend to think that cats are lazy critters. Au contraire! They are working hard on manufacturing not only important thoughts and dreams in their beta and REM time—they're conserving energy. Science in action indeed!

Zoology. Fred can name every small critter that lives in your yard, and he goes human scientists one better: he doesn't just examine and dissect, but he performs a taste test. Witness his expertise: he presents a small bundle of scientific evidence on the doorstep and says, "Meow," which, of course, in this context should be translated as *Passer domesticus*. He's not only identified a sparrow, but he knows its Latin name! Now it's just up to you to learn Cat Latin.

Literature

Unenlightened humans who look down on cats think they cannot read and are uninterested in books. We put this to you: Why do so many book owners have cats as well? Why do so many cats haunt bookstores and libraries? Why do cats curl up with you when you read a book? The answer: Feline Literary Osmosis. This process allows cats to absorb literature without having to perform the tiresome physical act of looking at the book and turning the pages. You sit down with, say, *Of Mice and Men* spread out before you, and Fred climbs aboard. Does it look as if he's just lying on the book, staring into the air? He's thinking about the symbolism. Doesn't symbolism give you a blank expression too?

Philosophy

The primary cat philosophy is contained in the Principle of the Eternal Meow. Alas, it is impossible for humans to totally embrace this profound concept, since only cats understand what it's like to be the focal point of time and space. However, with proper naps, treats, and soft couches, one day humans may achieve the serenity embodied by cats who practice the Eternal Meow.

Physics

Who's better at String Theory, you or Ginger? Need we say more?

Kitty Kulture

C ats are nothing if not refined, or so Fred and Ginger maintain. Wasn't it Fred, after all, who sang the line about "dustin' off my tails"? Granted, your Fred may not put on his top hat to go with his tail as Fred Astaire did, but in other ways he's a creature of high culture. You can honor all that culture by writing kitty haiku or using the Kitty Instant Story-Maker. Or get your kiterature ready-made: there's plenty to choose from.

And after you've seen the movie version, Fred and Ginger can enjoy their own videos. If you're really inspired, you can sing them kitty classics, then tour cat-happy sites around the globe. "Nothing more than we deserve!" says Ginger. "We *are* amused!"

Write Your Own Kitty Haiku

If cats could write poetry, there's a good chance they'd choose haiku: it's succinct and gets the job done without unnecessary frills. It's the lazy person's epic. But since cats can't write haiku, we can write it for them—and about them.

You probably remember from your school days that a haiku is an unrhymed three-line poem: the first line has five syllables, the second seven, and the third five again. So:

> *Cat in kitchen makes*
> *figure eight around ankles.*
> *Can opener love.*

Of course you can write cat haiku any time inspiration strikes, and pass it around to friends, inscribe it on cat cards (see chapter 4), post it on your Web site, or just keep it in a journal. But there's also a more communal way to write kitty haiku: Group Haiku. Group Haiku makes a good game at any party and is especially appropriate if you invite humans to your cat's birthday party (see chapter 5 for more on kitty birthday parties).

WHAT YOU'LL NEED:

- pens or pencils
- paper
- a group of friends (divided into threes)

Provide players with pencil and paper. Each will write one line of a kitty haiku, so count out the players according to the number of syllables allotted to each. The first player gets five syllables, the second seven syllables, the third five syllables; the fourth (beginning the next haiku) gets five syllables, the fifth seven syllables, the sixth five syllables, and so on. You may wish to announce a theme, such as "Irritating Cat Habits." Everyone writes his or her line without consulting the others. When all are done, go around the group and read the lines out in order. So the first player might write:

> *Always wanting treats.*

The second:

> *Loud meows at the crack of dawn.*

The third:

> *Walking on my face.*

What more artistic depiction of cat habits could even the great poets of yesteryear provide? As the example shows, the results will often follow a motif as if by magic, even though each line is written by a different person. You can also assign players a genre, such as "Hard-Boiled Detective" or "Western":

> *Chasin' varmints down:*
> *They called him Kitty the Kid.*
> *Six mice at high noon.*

Traditional haiku mention nature or a season, such as spring or fall, and purists may wish to follow this convention:

> *Kitties spring in air*
> *Leaping after butterflies,*
> *Heading for a fall.*

Okay, maybe that's not what the great poets meant by "spring" and "fall," but it's all about creativity, right?

"The Cat Came Back"
The Kitty Song Kollection

A chorus of cats isn't always melodious to the human ear, so instead we turn to songs about cats. You can sing these to Fred and Ginger while they're gathered in the kitchen waiting for dinner, or as they snuggle up beside you on the sofa waiting for you to provide an evening's entertainment. If your own singing isn't much beyond caterwauling, you might try Garrison Keillor's CD *Songs of the Cat*.

WHAT YOU'LL NEED:

- the following cat songs
- a kitty (or human) audience

Gather willing humans and serenade Fred and Ginger! The following cat-centered songs will get you started. Afterward, you can always try "Three Blind Mice."

"The Cat Came Back"

One of the best known of all cat songs, this ode to an indestructible cat was apparently written in 1893 by Harry S. Miller, in black dialect. It has since been transformed into a true folk song, existing in at least a dozen versions. This version was circulating in northern Wisconsin in the late '60s.

Old   Mis - ter   John - son   had   trou - bles   of   his   own.   He

had   a   yel - low   cat   that__   would - n't   leave   home_____   He did

ev - 'ry   thing   he   could   to   keep   the   cat   a - way.   He

gave   him   to   a   preach - er   and   he   told   him   for   to   stay____

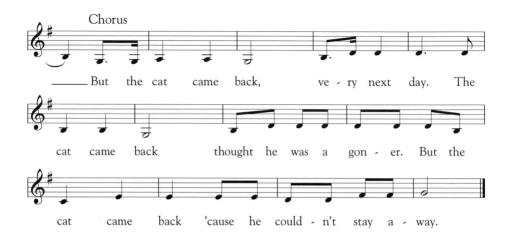

Chorus

But the cat came back, ve - ry next day. The
cat came back thought he was a gon - er. But the
cat came back 'cause he could - n't stay a - way.

He gave him to a man going up in a balloon,
Told him to give him to the man in the moon.
The balloon came down about twenty miles away
And where that man is now, nobody can say. BUT . . .

(Chorus)

The man around the corner said he'd shoot the cat on sight
So he loaded up his shotgun with nails and dynamite.
He waited and he waited for that cat to come around:
Ninety-seven pieces of the man were all they ever found.
 BUT . . .

(Chorus)

He gave him to a little boy with a dollar note.
He told the boy to take the cat upriver on a boat.
They tied a rock around his neck, must have weighed a hundred pound.
And now they're searching riverbanks for the little boy that drowned. BUT . . .

(Chorus)

They took him to a butcher shop with the butcher not around
And they dropped him in the hopper where the butcher's meat was ground.
The cat, he responded with a bloodcurdling shriek—
Our whole town's meat tasted bad for a week. BUT . . .

(Chorus)

[Slowly and mournfully]
The H-bomb fell just the other day.
The A-bomb fell in the very same way.
Russia went, China went, and the USA:
The human race was all destroyed without a chance to pray. [With energy]
    BUT . . .

(Chorus)

Want less violent fare? Try one of these:

Pussy-Cat, Pussy-Cat

Pus - sy - cat, pus- sy- cat, where have you been? I've been to Lon-don to vi -sit the Queen.

Pus - sy - cat, pus - sy- cat, what did you there? I frigh - ten'd a lit- tle mouse un- der her chair.

The Lazy Cat

Pus - sy, where have you been to -day?   In the mea - dows a - sleep in the hay,

Pus - sy, you are a   la - zy cat,   if you have done no more than that.

Films and Videos

Need something to keep you entertained between catnaps? One of these might be just the cat's pajamas.

The Top Cat Movies for Grown-ups

Harry and Tonto (1974)

ART CARNEY, ELLEN BURSTYN. Art Carney won an Oscar for this tale of a widower traveling cross-country with his cat, meeting disappointment and ultimately finding redemption.

Cat People (1942)

SIMONE SIMON, KENT SMITH, TOM CONWAY. This atmospheric B movie, directed by Jacques Tourneur, has gained cult status, and is about a woman who fears she belongs to an ancient race who turn into panthers when afflicted with jealousy. Moody and psychological. A gorier and altogether regrettable remake appeared under the same title in 1982, starring Nastassja Kinski and Malcolm McDowell.

Bell, Book, and Candle (1958)

KIM NOVAK, JAMES STEWART. Comedy about an attractive witch who uses her magical powers on an equally attractive man. Some parts of the story are seen through the eyes of her feline familiar, Pyewacket.

The Top Cat Movies for Kids

The Three Lives of Thomasina (1964)

PATRICK MCGOOHAN, SUSAN HAMPSHIRE. In this story of new life and hope, a little girl's cat is saved by a woman with unusual powers.

Born Free (1966)

VIRGINIA MCKENNA, BILL TRAVERS. The classic tale of Elsa the lioness, this movie is based on the true story recounted in Joy Adamson's book *Born Free*.

The Incredible Journey (1963)

EMILE GENEST, JOHN DRAINIE. A heartwarming story of a cat and two dogs making their way home through the wilderness.

Homeward Bound: The Incredible Journey (1993)

VOICES BY SALLY FIELD, MICHAEL J. FOX, DON AMECHE. That rare thing, a remake as good as the original. Again a cat and two dogs find their way through the wilderness; in this version we hear the animals' voices.

My Friend Totoro (1988)

One of the finest from Japanese master of animation Hayao Miyazaki. Two small girls move to the country with their father and soon learn about totoros, the friendly but mysterious spirits of the countryside. The totoros are somewhat cat-like, but this movie is especially worth seeing for the unforgettable cat bus that comes through the woods at night. The movie also appears under the title *My Neighbor Totoro*.

And, of course, there are a host of others, including *The Aristocats*, *Tom and Jerry*, *That Darn Cat!*, and *The Cat from Outer Space*, on up to *The Jungle Book* and *The Lion King*.

The Top Movies for Cats

But wait! Ginger doesn't want to watch a people video, with hours of boring plot and, what's worse, a lot of attention paid to some other cat. Instead she wants to watch just what she watches out the window: little quick-moving edible animals. Here is a selection of videos that provide just that, plus one (*The Adventures of Krazy Kats*) in which she can feel she's at an all-cat convention and pride herself on her resemblence to those lions.

Video Catnip, Cat TV, The Adventures of Betty Bird, The Adventures of Freddy Fish, The Adventures of Larry Lizard, The Adventures of Krazy Kats
Six videos for cats, featuring a host of leaping and skittering forms of tiny animal life.

Kitty Show Video Toy
A two-hour all-bugs video, featuring real bugs that appear to be crawling and fluttering on the TV screen.

Kitty Safari 1 and Kitty Safari 2
Birds, mice, critters, all doing what they do best.

CyberPounce
A digital film for cats that runs on your computer, with various fast-moving critters and toys.

Kitty-Happy Places to Visit

You may wish to experience kitty kulture more up close and personal than in the movies. There are cat museums and sights around the world. Be sure to check ahead for current admission days and times before planning your visit. Unfortunately, Fred and Ginger themselves aren't allowed in as sightseers. "I hate travel anyway," says Ginger. "Just send me a postcard and pick me up a souvenir can of tuna."

The Cat House (The Exotic Feline Breeding Compound's Feline Conservation Center)
Rosamond, California, U.S.A.

(661) 256-3332 (24-hour recorded directions and information)

Open 10 A.M.–4 P.M. every day except Wednesdays. Closed Christmas Day. Entrance fee.

www.cathouse-fcc.org

More than 50 of the world's endangered cats—including northern Chinese leopards, ocelots, margays, fishing cats, jaguars, tigers, and others—live in this nonprofit breeding zoo dedicated to helping endangered species.

Library Cats
www.ironfrog.com/catsmap.html

This unique website details the locale of all known cats living in libraries in the United States (including not only real cats but seven sculptures, one stuffed Siberian tiger, one stuffed mountain lion, and one virtual library cat). Cat access as close as your library!

Best Friends Animal Sanctuary

5001 Angel Canyon Road

Kanab, Utah 87741 U.S.A.

(435) 644-2001

www.bestfriends.com, visiting@bestfriends.org

Best Friends is the U.S.'s largest sanctuary for homeless and abused pets and domestic animals. A no-kill shelter, Best Friends houses at least 1,800 animals and, in addition to finding homes for adoptable animals, offers permanent homes for animals too old, crippled, or temperamentally unsuited to find homes as pets. Around 750 cats are housed at the Kitty Headquarters, the TLC Cat Club (for special-needs cats), and WildCats Village (for feral cats).

Best Friends is located on 350 acres in Angel Canyon, a red-rock canyon north of the Grand Canyon that has served as a backdrop for many films and TV shows, including *The Lone Ranger*. In addition to housing and finding homes for thousands of animals, Best Friends sponsors educational programs, offers a low-cost spay/neuter program for everyone who brings their pet in, and receives hundreds of volunteers who want to work with the animals for a day, several days, or longer.

Full information on visiting the sanctuary, including directions and accommodations, is available at *www.bestfriends.com/sanctuary/info/visitfaq.htm*. Visitors are welcome but are not allowed in the animal sanctuaries unaccompanied; guided tours are available by advance reservation: call (435) 644-2001, extension 0. Tours are free for members. Volunteers are always needed, and can work for one day or longer, but they need to make advance arrangements by calling the volunteer coordinator at (435) 644-2001, extension 119. Volunteers under 18 years old may work only upon approval of the staff, and must be accompanied by an adult at all times.

Torre Argentina Cat Sanctuary

Torre Argentina, Rome, Italy

http://home.wanadoo.nl/torre.argentina, torreargentina@yahoo.com

A cat sanctuary on the site where Brutus stabbed Julius Caesar in 44 B.C. The shelter, surrounded by ancient ruins, houses around 250 cats and is supported and staffed by volunteers from many countries.

Kattenkabinet (The Cat Cabinet)

Herengracht 497, Amsterdam, The Netherlands

Open Monday–Friday, 10 A.M.–2 P.M., Saturday and Sunday,

1–5 P.M. Entrance fee.

www.kattenkabinet.nl/html/index_engels_dhtml.html

A lovely collection of cat art and artifacts through the centuries.

The Cat Museum

Kuching, Sarawak, East Malaysia

Open Tuesday–Sunday, 9 A.M.–5 P.M.

www.sarawak.com.my/cat_museum/main.html

"Kuching" means "The Cat City," and the museum pays tribute to cats across the ages.

The Kitty Instant Story-Maker

Write your own customized kitty literature—and in the process, find out what's really on your cat's mind. Ginger says, "What do you think we're doing when we're out late howling at other cats? Gossiping, of course!"

WHAT YOU'LL NEED:

- pencil
- the following instant story
- friends to call out words for the story

WHAT YOU'LL DO:

Gather folks around and have them contribute words for the blanks as you ask for them (*without* reading them the story first). Then read the resulting masterpiece to the assembled crowd.

The Secret Diary of _____ , _____ Cat,
                 name of your cat   *praiseful adjective*

_____ . Again a day of triumphs and frustrations.
        today's date

_____ , the cat from down the street, came by to gossip
name of neighbor cat, or any cat name

about _____ , the new arrival over on _____ Street. She looks
     a female cat name   *local street*

so self-satisfied, but apparently she's just *covered* with _____ ! And not only that, but back
noun

where they used to live she had a litter of _____ kittens, and no tom in sight! The scandal!
number

Meanwhile, my quest to convince _____ that I need a dish of
your name

tuna every _____ hours has failed once again. It's _____,
number under 6   your cat's usual food

_____, _____, day in and day out! Don't they realize I am
same food   same food

a(n) _____, _____ beast whose every need must be _____ed?
adjective   another adjective   verb

I called the Society for the Prevention of Cruelty to Cats to report this outrage, but I

couldn't get through. _____ says they're busy handling the case of a family
neighbor cat's name

over in _____ who not only forbade their cat from sleeping on a nice pile of
nearby town

warm laundry, they opened a can of sardines and *didn't give their cat a single bite.* What is

the world coming to in these shocking times?

I am reassured by the fact that, although _____ is sadly misguided about
your name

the tuna, at least I have the _____ , the _____ , and a
your cat's favorite sleeping place   your cat's favorite toy

warm lap. In fact, I love _____ so much that I caught a _____
                                        your name   *small critter*

today and hid it in/under the _____ for _____ to find.
                                            hard-to-get-at place in your house   *your name*

When _____ next utters those incomprehensible words,
               your name

"_____" and "_____," I'll know what
       reprimand often given to cat   *another annoyed remark said to cat*

he/she really means: "You are the _____ of cats,
                                                    kind of royalty (king, princess, etc.)

_____, and no _____ cat has ever
        your cat's name   *praiseful adjective*

deserved a can of tuna more!"

A Tail of Two Kitties
A Selection of Great Cat Literature

Has the Instant Story-Maker inspired a thirst for more cat literature? Fortunately, there's great cat literature in every genre, from mysteries to poetry, from science fiction to tell-all exposés. And with a cat who loves to nap, there are opportunities for bedtime stories at every hour of the day. Here is a select list of volumes recommended by Fred and Ginger.

Cats in General

Dancing with Cats, by Burton Silver et al. They not only paint, they dance, as this tome demonstrates.

Everything Here Is Mine: An Unhelpful Guide to Cat Behavior, by Nicole Hollander. Cats' favorite jokes, the myth of the dainty eater, and more.

Great Cat Tales, edited by Lesley O'Mara. Cat stories from authors ranging from Mark Twain to Patricia Highsmith and James Herriot.

The New Roger Caras Treasury of Great Cat Stories, edited by Roger A. Caras.

The New Yorker Book of Cat Cartoons and *The New Yorker Book of All-New Cat Cartoons,* collections of classic New Yorker cartoons that feature cats.

Old Possum's Book of Practical Cats, by T. S. Eliot. One of the poetic masters turns his attention to one of the great subjects. This book of feline poetry inspired the musical *Cats*.

Poetry for Cats: The Definitive Anthology of Distinguished Feline Verse, edited by Henry Beard.

The Silent Miaow: A Manual for Kittens, Strays, and Homeless Cats, translated from the Feline by Paul Gallico. How to train your human—it all starts with the silent miaow.

The Sophisticated Cat: A Gathering of Stories, Poems, and Miscellaneous Writings About Cats, edited by Joyce Carol Oates and Daniel Halpern.

Why Cats Paint: A Theory of Feline Aesthetics, by Heather Busch et al. Didn't know cats could paint? This book shows they can—and how!

Feline Science Fiction and Fantasy

A Constellation of Cats, edited by Denise Little. Fantasy cat tales.

The Door into Summer, by Robert A. Heinlein. Petronius the Arbiter is a cat who just knows that, even if every other door leads to winter, the door into summer must be somewhere. In its noncat moments, the book is about time travel and a man with a problem. A favorite of Heinlein fans.

Time Cat: The Remarkable Journeys of Jason and Gareth, by Lloyd Alexander. A book for children ages 8 to 12, by the author of the popular *Chronicles of Prydain* series. Jason's cat, Gareth, can not only talk, he can travel through time, and the pair's many adventures range from ancient Egypt to Roman Britain to Revolutionary War America.

Cat Mysteries

Big Mike mysteries by Garrison Allen. Mystery-bookstore owner Penny Warren and her oversized cat Big Mike solve mysteries in Empty Creek, Arizona. Titles include **Dinosaur Cat**, **Movie Cat**, and others.

Cat series, by Lydia Adamson. Cat-sitter and sometime actress Alice Nestleton investigates mysteries with the help of her cats Bushy and Pancho. Titles include **A Cat in the Manger**, **A Cat of a Different Color**, and others.

The Cat Who . . . series by Lilian Jackson Braun, featuring mystery-solver Jim Qwilleran and his two Siamese helpers, Koko and Yum Yum. Titles include **The Cat Who Could Read Backwards**, **The Cat Who Ate Danish Modern**, **The Cat Who Played Post Office**, and others.

Crafty Cat Crimes: 100 Tiny Cat Tale Mysteries, edited by Stefan Dziemianowicz, Robert Weinberg, and Martin H. Greenberg. Cat mysteries of all kinds by a variety of authors.

Joe Grey mysteries by Shirley Rousseau Murphy. Joe Grey and Dulcie are cats who have the remarkable ability to talk, read, use the phone—and, of course, solve mysteries. Titles include **Cat on the Edge**, **Cat in the Dark**, **Cat to the Dogs**, and others.

Midnight Louie mysteries by Carole Nelson Douglas. Midnight Louie and his human, Temple Barr, do some hard-boiled sleuthing in Las Vegas. Titles include **Catnap**, **Pussyfoot**, **Cat on a Blue Monday**, and others.

Mrs. Murphy mysteries by Rita Mae Brown (written with the help of her cat, Sneaky Pie

Brown). A cat, Mrs. Murphy, teams up with three sidekicks (a dog, a cat, and a human) to solve mysteries. Titles include **Pawing Through the Past**, **Claws and Effect**, **Murder, She Meowed**, and others.

Marian Babson's cat mysteries, featuring a Maine coon cat named Errol. Titles include **Nine Lives to Murder**, **Whiskers and Smoke**, and others.

A Treasury of Cat Mysteries, edited by Martin H. Greenberg.

A Kitty Soap Opera
A Choose-Your-Own-Adventure Tail

For this choose-your-own-adventure tail, cast your own kitty or kitties and any of your friends or neighbors' cats you like—no tryouts necessary! Is your cat the intrepid Tom Mouser, the sleek Kitty Treats, the relentless "Fat Cat" Basso Profundo, the noble Tuna Profundo, or the free spirit Liver Treats? As you read, you'll ask your cat for directions on which plot to choose at the decision points. So summon your kitty helpers and embark on the saga of Tom and Kitty and a day in the life of Port Sandbox.

Nine Lives to Live
Romance, Adventure, Furballs

CAST:

Tom Mouser: Tom roams the world as a secret agent for P.A.W.S.—Pet Alliance for World Security. Although he has been on assignment in remote parts of the globe for the past ten years, his heart still belongs to:

Kitty Treats: Sex kitten turned nurse, Kitty treated Tom in General Vet Hospital after he used three lives battling the forces of S.N.A.R.L. (Secret Notorious Agents, Rogues, and Layabouts). They married, and soon the patter of little paws graced their lives.

Basso Profundo: Known as "Fat Cat" to friends and enemies, Basso is a don in the Growlfia, the disorganized crime league. His son:

Tuna Profundo: is a graduate of Meowford University, a scientist working with patients at General Vet to find a cure for furballs. He is in love with:

Liver Treats: lead singer in the punk band the Hissy Fits, and daughter of Tom and Kitty.

With a special cameo by Fred!

Episode No. 4692

—————————————●1●—————————————

Tom Mouser leapt into the shadows of the Port Sandbox hospital building. He had only been back in Port Sandbox for three hours, and already someone was following him! He thanked his lucky stars that he had chosen to go out in black today, as he did every day.

The figure turned. It hissed. It had seen him!

Tom pounced. A collar tag jingled as he took the enemy down. Using kat jitsu, he pinned it—and pulled off the mask.

The moon that rode above the harbor shone down on a sleek golden fur coat. Tom gasped.

It was none other than Kitty Treats, the wife he had not seen in ten years.

Decision point: What does Tom do? Consult your cat by patting him.

*If your cat acts content, that means Tom Mouser is at ease
     with the situation. Go to section 2.*

*If your cat gets up, that means Tom Mouser senses danger.
     He takes a swing at Kitty Treats. Go to section 7.*

———————————————●2●———————————————

"Darling, I heard you'd gone back to Catalonia to stay with your mother! What an unexpected treat to see you!" purred Mouser. He rubbed his nose tenderly against hers.

"Unhand me, you agent of evil!" cried Kitty Treats with a low growl.

"Kitty, don't you recognize me? Tom Mouser, your husband." Even after all this time, love flamed in his breast hotter than heartburn after a garbage-can dinner.

"Tom? Where have you been for ten years?" gasped Kitty, the growl subsiding.

He cleared his throat—another dang furball had gotten stuck in there. How could he tell her the whole story? He'd had a job in Port Sandbox as the head of an international mackerel cartel, but P.A.W.S. had begged him to take one more assignment, to help rid this dog-eat-dog world of evil. One thing led to another, and almost before he knew it ten years had passed. Despite the passage of time, he had never stopped yearning for the woman he had left behind.

"I've been ridding the world of evil—it took longer than I thought it would. Right now I'm here to save Port Sandbox from the claws of the Growlfia. But why are you lurking in the alleys like this, my darling?"

"Actually, I've taken a job with the Growlfia—"

> **Decision point: What does Tom do on hearing she's working for the evil Growlfia? Consult your cat by rubbing him under the chin.**
> *If your cat starts to purr, it means Tom is calm enough to listen to Kitty's story about the Growlfia. Go to section 3.*
> *If your cat moves his head aside in annoyance, it means Tom needs to be concerned about Kitty's loyalties. Tom takes a swing at her. Go to section 7.*

———————— 3 ————————

"You work for Fat Cat and the Growlfia?" asked Tom, shuddering with memories of too many agents who had disappeared under the weight of cement collars. "But they're evil!"

"No, listen!" said Kitty. She pushed her fur coat back to reveal a black jumpsuit. He couldn't help but notice that she hadn't lost any of her lithe kittenish figure. "The Growlfia thinks they've hired me, but I'm undercover—I'm actually working for the Feline Bureau of Investigation. Why do you think I'm skulking around the hospital, spying? I thought you were an operative for some other evil organization."

Tom eyed her. He felt a purr trembling through his body. Ten years on, this babe was still the cat's meow. "No—still working for P.A.W.S. I'm sorry I ever had to leave Port Sandbox, Kitty."

As he pulled her close, a purr began to rise in her throat, but then she pushed him away.

"There's something you should know, Tom. After two years of grieving, I moved on. I married your best friend, Fred."

Tom took a deep breath. "He and Ginger got divorced?"

"It's a long soap opera, Tom. You should have stayed around. And your daughter Liver Treats sings in a punk band called the Hissy Fits. Of course it sounds more like yowling than singing. She's been seeing Dr. Tuna Profundo, son of Basso Profundo, the Growlfia Boss."

Tom yowled with outrage. "Where is this rat?"

"Why, he's in the hospital lab, researching a cure for furballs, Tom. But don't—"

Tom threw open the door of the hospital and bounded into the research lab. There, among scientific equipment and catfood dishes, in a white smock, was the young and handsome Dr. Profundo. Dr. Profundo smoothed his whiskers and stared at Tom.

Decision Point: What does Tom do upon confronting the son of the Growlfia boss who's dating his daughter? Consult your cat by dangling a string in front of him.

If your cat ignores the string, it means Tom is determined to act cautiously.
He begins by expressing his feelings to Dr. Profundo—and demanding that he cure his furball problem. Go to section 4.

If your cat grabs the string, it means Tom is determined to act decisively. He belts Dr. Profundo in the puss. Go to section 7.

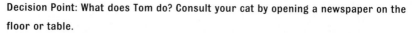

"Dr. Profundo," said the secret agent. "My daughter's too good for a lowlife like you. I warn you to stay away from her! Also, I've got a terrible furball I can't get up. Can you give me something?"

The doctor nodded. "For the furball I suggest my latest invention, Balls-Up." The doctor handed Tom a smoking beaker. "As for Liver—you'll have to tell her yourself."

A sleek and fangsome feline in leather strode from the elevator, electric guitar slung around her neck.

"Daddy! After all this time! You look like something the cat dragged in!"

Decision Point: What does Tom do? Consult your cat by opening a newspaper on the floor or table.

If your cat stays where he is, it means Tom wants to get back to normal. He swallows his pride—and his furball—and tries to reunite with his daughter Liver. Go to section 5.

If your cat gets up and sits on the newspaper, it means Tom loses his temper and takes action. Hurt and offended, he takes a swing at Liver Treats. Go to section 7.

5

Tom straightened his whiskers and rubbed a paw over his ear self-consciously. "Liver. You've grown up!" said Tom, swallowing back his emotion—or was it that blasted furball?

"Daddy!" Liver Treats put her paws to her leather sides and glared. "You don't know the trouble you caused in Port Sandbox when you left. You didn't even leave a note—we had to start from scratch. We suspected it was some kind of government cover-up."

"I'm sorry, baby. I've been working for the cause of justice, truth, and clean litter boxes for all."

"Hold it!" said Dr. Profundo. "My timer has just gone off! If the formula is correct, this latest batch will not only cure furballs, but have a delightful fishy bouquet as well. This could be the key to worldwide harmony and cleanliness!"

Before he could test the new medicine, the door burst open.

Five cats smoking cigars and wearing coats around their shoulders hunkered in, led by an enormous tiger-striped cat, dressed in a Maine coon coat, with one ragged ear.

"Fat Cat!" said Tom.

Decision Point: What does Tom do? Consult your cat by holding out a kitty treat.

If your cat remains quiet, it means Tom tries diplomatic means to deal with the Growlfia. Go to section 6.

If your cat meows, it means Tom decides on action and bops Fat Cat in the nose. Go to section 7.

"Fat Cat," said Tom. "You've been tailing me, haven't you? But maybe we can still reach an agreement."

"Fuggeddaboutit," growled the Growlfia chieftain. "I got more important things to deal with than P.A.W.S." He turned to his son. "You got a great life ahead of you, Tuna-face. Why are ya messin' with lowlifes like Liver Treats and punk bands?"

Dr. Profundo gathered the leather-clad Liver into his arms. "But I love her, father."

The elevator dinged. The doors opened to reveal Kitty Treats and a group of Feline Bureau of Investigation agents. They poured out of the elevator, brandishing guns.

"You're all under arrest," she cried.

"That's right!" said Tom's former best friend, Fred, in a trenchcoat. "I'm the new chief of police here in Port Sandbox . . . and I'm arresting you all. Including you, Tom Mouser!"

> Decision Point: What happens next? Consult your cat by giving him a dish of tuna.
>
> *If he eats it and demands more, it means Tom is still fired up. He takes a swing at Fred. Go to section 7.*
>
> *If your cat eats the tuna and then washes himself contentedly, it means the episode is over for today. Episode 4693 will take place tomorrow, when Fred and Tom face off over Kitty's affection, and the fur begins to fly! Now stay tuned for The Young and the Frisky.*

The body fell to the floor, out cold.

Tom looked down at it.

Fade to Balls-Up Furball Creme commercial.

Kitty Krafts

Superior as cats are in almost every way—as they will tell you themselves—they lack one essential trait: opposable thumbs. This means they rely on us for essential kitty krafts such as growing catnip and sewing it into mice, not to mention putting together necessities like window perches and cat trees. Think cats are not so superior after all? Guess who they're getting to do all the work!

Don't worry—Ginger will supervise!

Gardening with Your Cat (Catnip and Beyond)

And lately, when I was not feeling fit,
Bereft alike of Piety and Wit,
There came an Angel Shape and offered me
A fragrant Plant and bid me taste of it.

'Twas that reviving Herb, that Spicy Weed
The Cat-Nip. Tho' 'tis good in time of need,
Ah, feed upon it lightly, for who knows
To what unlovely antics it may lead.

—Oliver Herford, *The Rubaiyat of a Persian Kitten* (1904)

Catnip for Cats

Why are cats always scratching in the dirt? Could it be they're hinting at something? Such as, "Sow that catnip now, bud!"?

Catnip is the paws-down winner for best-loved plant, turning many a sedate puss into a rolling, purring, happily drunken fool for love. The secret is nepetalactone, a component as appealing to lions and leopards as it is to Fred Housecat. Domestic kittens, however, don't get the catnip habit until they're two to three months old, and one out of three cats never understands what all the fuss is about.

Catnip is easy to grow, and there are a host of lesser-known garden plants also attractive to cats. Catnip (*Nepeta cataria*) is a member of the mint family; it has gray-green leaves and small white or lavender flowers.

WHAT YOU'LL NEED:

- catnip seeds (you can find seeds in plant nurseries or in some pet stores)
- a sunny space in the garden (for outdoor plants)
- a pot or windowbox and good potting soil (for indoor plants)

WHAT YOU'LL DO:

1. For outdoor plants, sow the seeds as directed on the package; choose a sunny place in your garden in the spring. For indoor plants, sow seeds in a pot or windowbox full of good potting soil; place in a sunny window. Water enough to keep soil somewhat moist but not soggy.

2. The seeds will take up to 21 days to germinate. If the plants are spaced too closely, thin them by uprooting extraneous seedlings until the remaining plants are spaced around 15 inches (38 cm) apart. It may be that Ginger and her friends will perform this task for you. If the Ginger catnip posse is interfering with the crop too greatly, protect plants with a wire cage.

3. Once the plants have begun to flower, cut the stems back to eight inches (20 cm) and strip the leaves off. The stems will grow back, and, as they're perennials, the plants will continue year after year, provided the catnip posse is restrained.

4. Dry the leaves on a tray or cookie sheet in a secure cat-proof area for two to four weeks, until the dried leaves crumble easily. (Discard the stems, which are not cat appealing.)

5. Once the leaves have dried, store them in an airtight bag or jar and dispense at will.

Catnip for Humans

If you want to share in the experience as best a poor nepetelactone-impaired human can, while Ginger is rolling and purring you can partake of a cup of catnip tea.

WHAT YOU'LL NEED:

- dried catnip, preferably homegrown or organic (regular pet shop catnip is not high enough grade for human consumption)
- teapot
- tea strainer
- boiling water
- cup

Put two to three heaping teaspoonfuls of dried catnip in a teapot, pour boiling water in, and let steep for 5 to 10 minutes. Pour the tea through a tea strainer into your cup.

Catnip tea is said to settle the stomach, but however minty and good it is, it will not, alas, have you rolling on the kitchen floor.

Other Cat Pleasers

There are a number of other plants pleasing to cats. Try one or more of the following:

Catmint (*Nepeta faassenii* and its smaller sister *Nepeta mussinii*). This plant is related to catnip but makes a more picturesque ground cover, with white, blue, or lavender flowers. Plant in the same manner as catnip; your cats will soon show you if catmint is strong enough for them.

Cat thyme (*Teucrium marum*). Actually not related to thyme, but to germander, it is a variety of mint, like catnip and catmint. Cat thyme is a shrubby plant with red flowers, a lover of sun and drought-tolerant—perhaps the perfect cat-appealing plant to the brown thumbs among us. There's no need to cut or dry the plant; cats will make their own fun gnawing on the leaves as the plant grows.

Valerian (*Valeriana officinalis*). Sometimes called garden heliotrope (although it's not related to other heliotropes), valerian is a large herb that can reach four feet, with tiny, sweet-smelling flowers in a variety of colors. Plant in sun or part shade, and prepare for valerian to grow and spread vigorously—another boon for the garden-impaired! The flowers also look nice in indoor bouquets, especially if you don't mind Fred on the table.

Wheatgrass. This easy-to-grow plant is especially good in windowboxes. See Chapter 7.

Last, if you want to flatter Fred rather than intoxicate him, you could plant cat's-claw (*Macfadyena unguis-cati*), cat's-ears (*Calochortus tolmei*), cat's-foot (*Antennaria dioica*), pussytoes (*Antennaria arcuata*), pussy ears (*Cyanotis somaliensis*), pussy willow (*Salix discolor*), or cattails (*Typha*).

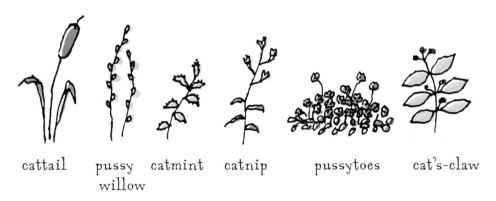

cattail   pussy   catmint   catnip   pussytoes   cat's-claw
           willow

Make Catnip Toys

With your homegrown catnip, or with the store-bought variety, you can concoct a number of toys that will keep Fred happy for hours. Try a mouse or a catfish, or let Santa bring Fred his catnip in a stocking.

Making a Catnip Mouse

WHAT YOU'LL NEED:

- a square of felt or sturdy fabric, 4 inches x 4 inches (10 cm x 10 cm)
- scissors
- needle and thread
- laundry marker (an indelible marker that will write on clothing)
- 3 ½-inch (9 cm) length of string
- catnip to fill mouse, the more recently bought or dried the better
- dried lentils (optional)
- piece of pink fabric about 2 inches x 2 inches (5 cm x 5 cm) square (optional)

WHAT YOU'LL DO:

Enlarge the pattern at right using a photo-copier. Trace the outline of the mouse onto the felt or fabric.

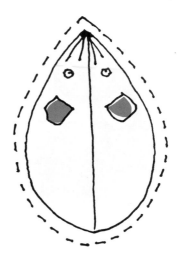

Cut out the mouse from the fabric. Fold the outline in half along the mouse's belly to make a mouse shape, putting the right sides (the sides that will end up outside) together. Starting where the back feet would be, stitch the mouse together, going around the outline and stopping when the mouse's back is nearly done. Turn the mouse right-side out. Stuff it full of catnip. If you do not have enough catnip, include a few dried lentils to fill it out. Insert the string where the tail should be and stitch the mouse completely closed, being sure to secure the string in place as you stitch. Use a laundry marker to draw ears, eyes, and whiskers. Or for those with deluxe mouse ambitions, trace the shape of two ears on the square of pink fabric, cut out, and sew to sides of the mouse's head.

Finally, scrunch the mouse between your fingers a few times to release the catnip scent, and call Ginger.

Making a Catnip Catfish

WHAT YOU'LL NEED:

• the same materials as required for the catnip mouse, minus the string

WHAT YOU'LL DO:

Enlarge the pattern below using a photocopier. Trace the outline of the fish onto the felt or fabric, and follow the instructions as for the catnip mouse, except, obviously, for the string tail. Use laundry marker to draw eyes.

Making a Catnip Sock

When Ginger hangs her stockings up by the fire, let's hope they're filled with catnip and not with coal! You can help fulfill this desire by making a catnip sock.

WHAT YOU'LL NEED:

- an infant sock
- catnip
- length of ribbon
- dried lentils (optional)

WHAT YOU'LL DO:

Begin with an infant sock: if it's used, make sure it's clean. Stuff with catnip or, if you need extra filler, with catnip and a few dried lentils. Tie closed tightly with ribbon not far above the heel, knotting ribbon a number of times and leaving the ends dangling enticingly. For extra kitty appeal, use a sock rattle, a baby sock that comes with a rattle on the toes. Between the rattling and the smell of catnip, Ginger will be in seventh heaven!

Make a Scratching Post

If you don't provide a scratching post for your cats, they may well provide one for themselves, in the form of a scratching sofa or a scratching chair. A genuine post, on the other hand, satisfies Ginger's instinct to scratch and your instinct to tinker and make things—satisfaction all round!

WHAT YOU'LL NEED:

- one wooden post, at least 30 inches (76 cm) tall and 4 inches (10 cm) wide
- one piece of carpet, as long as the post and wide enough to fit all the way around post
- heavy scissors to cut carpet
- one piece of plywood, at least 16 inches x 16 inches (40 cm x 40 cm), to form base
- four galvanized nails, 3 inches (8 cm) long or more
- hammer
- staple gun and staples sturdy enough to staple through carpet, or small nails
- catnip

WHAT YOU'LL DO:

Measure the carpet so it fits all the way around the post with minimal overlap and just covers the top of the post. Cut carpet. Wrap the carpet around the post, stapling in the rear along the seam. (If the carpet is especially thick, you may wish to nail it rather than staple it to the post.) Fold carpet down over the top of the post and staple neatly. Attach the post to the base by hammering galvanized nails through the

bottom of the base, up into the post. Test for sturdiness. Rub catnip into carpet to give your cat the idea that this is an attractive new addition to the household. Voilà—a new scratching post.

Make a Kitty Catstle

WHAT YOU'LL NEED:

- one or more large sturdy cardboard boxes
- X-acto knife or other cutting implement
- wooden boards of any size suitable to be used as cat ramps (optional)

WHAT YOU'LL DO:

If the box has a lid, cut it off, and turn the box upside down. Now cut a cat-sized entrance in two or more sides of the box, one at floor level, another higher up. (If you have a mother cat and kittens, cut one large entrance for the mother and several smaller ones for the kittens—first she'll try to follow them in the kitten-sized entrances, and finally go in her own adult-sized one.) Cats will have fun with only one Catstle, but they'll have an even better time if there are also outlying boxes. If you have a second box, cut a floor-level entrance in it and another entrance higher up, level with the higher-up entrance of the first box. Then lay the board between the boxes, resting on the bottom sill of each exit. (For the "good old boy" method of securing the board, use duct tape.) With additional boards, make ramps up to other high-level Catstle entrances. With a good supply of boxes and boards, you can take up a whole living room with a Catstle extravaganza. A kitty's home is his Catstle!

Make a Cat Room

Fred and Ginger say that if you love them *very* much, you'll modify a whole room for their enjoyment. This means a perch for every window and scratching posts and cat trees spread liberally around. For a truly deluxe cat retreat, install upper-level cat paths: carpeted shelves stretching the length of a whole wall, about two feet from the ceiling, with a network of catwalks, at the same level, crisscrossing the room. Of course you'll need cat staircases to get up to that level: either build your own or carpet a stepladder with wide rungs, and make sure it won't shift under the weight of cats bounding up and down it. Then position some Kitty Catstles on the floor and a few gooseneck lamps pointing down onto soft beds.

"Wonderful!" says Ginger. "I'll just ring for the butler to bring me some tuna . . ."

Make Kitty Kards and T-Shirts

Cards and T-shirts follow the same basic pattern: Ginger does the artwork and you add an appropriate quotation. (Of course, to simplify things, you could use only the artwork or only the quotation. But then you and Ginger wouldn't be crafting together.)

WHAT YOU'LL NEED:

For cards:

- good-quality stiff white paper
- nontoxic stamp pads, in black or colors
- colored pens
- newspaper
- cat treats
- damp sponge

For T-shirts:

- T-shirt paint (available in craft stores)
- plain white T-shirts
- paintbrushes
- newspaper
- cat treats
- damp sponge

WHAT YOU'LL DO:

For the cards, measure and cut out the size card you'd like. A good size for a large card is 5 inches by 7 inches (13 cm by 18 cm), for which you'll need to cut a square 10 inches by 14 inches (26 cm by 36 cm), so you can fold the card in half. For a small card, a good size is 3 1/2 inches by 5 inches (9 cm by 13 cm), for which you'll need to cut a square 7 inches by 10 inches (18 cm by 36 cm). Or get out your envelopes, measure them, and cut out a square twice as large, so that when you finish the cards you'll have envelopes guaranteed to fit.

The T-shirt requires no preparation. If you get it out ahead of time, however, Ginger may decide to nap on it, which will get her ready for more purposeful T-shirt attention.

Now you're ready to decorate the card or T-shirt. If neither you nor Ginger is an accomplished artist, Pawprint Art is the way to go. Begin in the kitchen. Spread the newspaper on the floor (this is to prevent Ginger from tracking ink all over) and get out the cat treats. At the appearance of the cat treats, Ginger should be quite atten-tive. For Classic Black & White Pawprint Art, just bring Ginger's front paws (gently!) to the stamp pad or a small saucer of T-shirt paint, then induce her to step on the front of the card or T-shirt, using the treats as bait.

For Color Pawprint Art, have your colored inkpad ready. If you're making a T-shirt, prepare several saucers with different colors of T-shirt paint. Again, apply ink or paint to Ginger's front paws and bait her onto the card or T-shirt. Supply cat treats aplenty.

Once Ginger has contributed her pawprint, swab the bottom of her paws with the damp sponge to remove the ink or paint. Although the substances are nontoxic, you really don't want her licking it off and swallowing it.

Let the cards or T-shirt dry, and then apply your own sayings with the colored pens or T-shirt paint. For the cards, your message could be simple, such as "Ginger and I are thinking of Pouncer and you" or "Happy Birthday! You're the cat's meow!" or "Paws and take a break—you deserve it!" A T-shirt might sport a similarly basic motto, such as "MY CAT WALKS ALL OVER ME!" Or you could go classic and inscribe a cat quotation. Below are some of Ginger's favorites.

There are no ordinary cats.
> —Colette

If man could be crossed with the cat, it would improve mankind but deteriorate the cat.
> —Mark Twain

One cat just leads to another.
> —Ernest Hemingway

Dogs come when they're called; cats take a message and get back to you.
  —Mary Bly

Are cats lazy? Well, more power to them if they are. Which one of us has not entertained the dream of doing just as he likes, when and how he likes, and as much as he likes?
  —Fernand Méry

When I play with my cat, who knows whether I do not make her more sport than she makes me?
  —Michel de Montaigne

It is a very inconvenient habit of kittens (Alice had once made the remark) that, whatever you say to them, they always purr.
  —Lewis Carroll

God made the cat in order that man might have the pleasure of caressing the lion.
  —Fernand Méry

It is impossible to keep a straight face in the presence of one or more kittens.
  —Cynthia E. Varnado

Cats, no less liquid than their shadows,
Offer no angles to the wind.
They slip, dimished, neat, through loopholes
Less than themselves.
  —A. S. J. Tessimond

The Litterbox as Zen Garden

Miniature Zen gardens have become one of the latest home accessories, a little oasis of calm in the midst of the everyday bustle. With the litterbox Zen garden, you and Ginger can partake of inner peace! The typical miniature Zen garden is, tellingly, about the size of a litterbox, and consists of fine sand or grit, raked into soothing patterns, with a few stones placed here and there for contrast. (If you're interested in Zen gardens as a concept, you might consult A. K. Davidson's *The Art of Zen Gardens* or Philip Cave's *Creating Japanese Gardens*. Neither Davidson nor Cave is on the cutting edge of the litterbox garden movement, however.) As you'll see, a Zen garden is already halfway to being a litterbox and a litterbox is already halfway to being a Zen garden.

WHAT YOU'LL NEED:

- a litterbox
- kitty litter
- litter scoop

WHAT YOU'LL DO:

If you have an indoor cat, you already have the litterbox, and if it's full of kitty litter, you already have the grit. A litterbox scoop serves as a dandy Zen rake. Now just rake the grit into pleasing patterns. Breathe in, breathe out. Think nice, calming thoughts.

The final touch to the Zen garden is the larger rocks, typically water-polished, smooth rocks. These might be a liability in the litterbox. We hesitate to suggest that your cat will provide a substitute for these—perhaps it would just be best to say that nature will supply everything appropriate to the Zen litterbox. And then you'll have a reason to use the rake/scoop every day!

Ahhh . . . nothing like a Zen litterbox to bestow inner peace . . .

Cat Photography

Of course you'll want photos to commemorate Fred's kittenhood, graduation from mouser school, catnip antics, and general adorability. You can assemble a special cat photo album, post Fred's pictures on his Web site, or put together a collage for the Kitty Birthday Party.

WHAT YOU'LL NEED:

- a camera
- film (unless you're using a digital camera)
- your cat in many photogenic poses

WHAT YOU'LL DO:

Photograph your cat in a variety of moods and antics. Follow these tips for superior pictures:

Seize the opportunity. Have the camera ready in a handy spot, so you can capture an especially appealing pose without having to hunt through cabinets for the camera.

Go for close-ups. For best results, use a more expensive camera (for instance, not a disposable) so you can focus in on your cat. Cheaper cameras often cannot focus on subjects closer than three feet. At a distance of three feet, Fred can look mighty small in the picture. Go for close-ups instead.

Try an action sequence. Have someone else dangle a string for Fred, or embark on the Changing-the-Sheets Game (see page 6), and then snap a sequence of photos as the game unfolds.

Include yourself. Have someone take photos of you with Fred: playing with string, on your lap, on your shoulder. Then you have a nice pretext for sending pictures of Fred to all your friends and relatives, and for putting them on kitty kards. They can also work well if you happen to need publicity photos (for your latest real estate promotion or the Nobel Prize)—people warm to folks with a pet in their lives.

Experiment. For classic appeal, try shooting a roll of film in black and white—it can give Fred a whole new artistic look. Or catch Fred as a blur as he dashes across the room. Get down on the floor and take photos from cat's-eye level. Experiment with styles, angles, and poses—the sky's the limit!

Catdoor Fun

If your cat goes outside, and you've been letting him or her out yourself, a catdoor can save enormous time and trouble. Catdoor technology has advanced to the point where doors can be installed in sliding glass doors, and keyed so that only your cat can operate the door (via a sensor on his or her collar), which keeps out neighborhood cats and other curious beasts. Ready-made catdoors can be bought in most pet stores or by mail order. Unless you have woodworking or construction experience, you'll want to let a handyman or other professional install the door (instructions will come in the package). But a working catdoor is only the beginning: a catdoor worthy of Fred and Ginger will be not only functional but decorative. One of the following ideas might be just the cat's meow.

WHAT'LL YOU NEED:

- a catdoor
- decorations (as detailed below)
- nails, paint, glue, or other aids to decoration

WHAT YOU'LL DO:

Choose an idea and make your catdoor a festive entrance. You can even change the decor by the season.

Celebrate the season. If you have a swinging catdoor (as opposed to the kind made of many separate flaps), you can hang seasonal decorations on it to match the decorations on your own front door: a wreath for wintertime, perhaps, or the silhouette of a black cat for Halloween. Of course, make sure any wreaths you put up are

nontoxic to cats, and don't put up a catnip wreath unless you want the whole
neighborhood cat posse gathered
around the catdoor.

Put up a picture. Glue up an appropriate
picture, whether drawn or cut out from
a magazine. Or simply enlarge a photo
of Ginger. The hind end of a cat, glued
up as if disappearing through the door,
says it all.

Try trompe l'oeil. Paint or glue a trompe l'oeil picture on the catdoor. From the inside,
the picture could be of the outside: the lawn or scenery just beyond the catdoor. From
the outside, the picture will be of the inside: the floor or cabinet just beyond the door.
It is not nice to put up a picture of the neighborhood bully cat peering in.

The cosmic catdoor. Make the catdoor part of a grander cosmic scheme. Medieval
artists depicted the entrance to hell as the mouth of a giant beast, gaping wide. Paint
a hellmouth around your catdoor, with the door itself the entrance to the nether-
world (maybe a nice warning to Ginger about where she'll go if she scratches the sofa
one more time?). An appropriate kitty hell-beast would look something like a cat,
maybe with a few sinner mice underneath her claws. A dramatic painting like this
should have an inscription above it, perhaps painted on an authoritative-looking
scroll, something like ABANDON MICE, ALL YE WHO ENTER HERE.

If the hellmouth is too formidable, you could imagine a heavenmouth: a smiley Cheshire-cat-looking beast with catnip under her claws. Or if you wanted to suggest the Great Beyond in a more abstract way, you could just paint the catdoor a nice dark blue with stars.

Create Your Own Website About Your Cat

Millions of humans have their own websites—don't Fred and Ginger deserve one too? In fact, they'll be joining the ranks of hundreds of cats whose exploits are celebrated on the Web. Let Ginger sit in your lap as you're constructing your website; then she gets lap time while you get computer time. (If she's like many other cats, she may also want to sit on the keyboard, which may result in some key-pressing and letters being typed on the screen. Feel free to delete these—although she's eloquent in person, Ginger's written prose style is atrocious.) When you need to take a break from complex computer programming, try moving the cursor around on the screen and see if Ginger wants to chase it. Or you could acquire the more sophisticated computer version of the moving cursor, the computer cat-game CyberPounce (see Videos in Chapter 3 and the Resources section on page 121). Constructing a website can take quite a while, and frequent fun-breaks are good for both you and Ginger!

- a computer
- a server
- text for the website
- graphics for the website

Think about all the elements and how they will go together.

The server. The server is the computer that hosts the site. Many people find that their Internet service provider offers them free or cheap webpage storage, as well as, in some cases, step-by-step create-your-own-website tools. Check with your Internet service provider to see if this is true in your case. Some larger companies offer free websites. One of the most popular of these, for instance, is *Geocities.yahoo.com*. These commercial sites may offer more storage space; possible disadvantages are that they will probably put a pop-up ad on your site, and that, unlike many smaller local providers, they may not offer a free helpline.

The text. What do you want your website to say? You might include:

▸ an introduction to yourself and your cats

▸ the story of how you found or came to meet your cats

▸ your cat haiku or other poetry

- your thoughts about anything in the cat world: favorite cat books, cat breeds, cat toys, cat philosophy

- captions for photos

- links to other important catsites (important to you, such as stray cat rescue guidelines; or important to Fred, such as the website for that attractive tabby down the street)

The graphics. Last, what's a catsite without pictures? If you have a flatbed scanner, you can scan your photos into a digital format so they can be used on your site. If not, many commercial computer and photocopying stores can do it for you for a small fee. Or you can have traditional photos saved to CD and upload them to your website. Choose your most flattering photos of Fred and Ginger and let the world envy you! There are also a number of sites on the Web where you can download free cat graphics (clip art, backgrounds, icons, and more) for your website: one such is CatStuff, at *www.xmission.com/~emailbox/catstuff.htm.*

Once you've composed or chosen the text for your site, you'll need to get it into HTML, the formatting that allows it to be read comfortably on screen. There are many programs that translate plain text into HTML, such as Netscape Composer (bundled in with Netscape) or Microsoft FrontPage, which is often bundled in with Office software. Microsoft Word also lets you save pages in HTML format. If you have that adventurous spirit, you can also teach yourself HTML fairly quickly. Two online sites to instruct you are the Bare Bones Guide to HTML, at *http://werbach.com/barebones/download.html*, and HTML Goodies, at *http://htmlgoodies.com*. Or if you prefer the traditional method, try a book such as Bud Smith and Arthur Beback's *Creating Web Pages for Dummies* or Steve Callihan's *Create Your First Web Page in a Weekend*.

Once your text and graphics are ready, you'll need to transfer the file from your computer to the site where it will be stored, whether at your Internet service provider, Geocities, or elsewhere. This varies somewhat according to which ISP you've picked; its help pages will guide you.

For a truly deluxe website, you can even set up a webcam to broadcast your cat's every move—or as many as the webcam will capture. For this you will need a webcam as well as a cable modem or DSL line to transmit images rapidly. Here we move beyond the scope of beginners; consult a computer expert to determine exactly what products fit your needs.

Kooking for Kitty and Other Celebrations

A special meal makes any day a celebration, and kitty kuisine goes far beyond food scooped out of a can. Here are a number of meals, both simple and deluxe, to turn any day into Fred and Ginger Day. You can go all out for kitty birthdays—even humans can partake of special foods that do homage to the feline members of the household. And when the holidays roll around, there's no need for Fred and Ginger to mope on the sidelines. They can ward off mice and sea monsters on St. Gertrude's Day, eat Mackereltaschen on Purrim, frolic like the sprites they are on Midsummer Eve, and test out that cold white stuff on First Snow-on-the-Paws Day. "And please note," says Fred, "the instructions for Endless Lap Day. Any day can be Endless Lap Day—what about today?"

Kitty Favorite Foods You Might Not Know

The Standard Law of Kitty Konsumption: All wet food is better than all dry food, and all strong-smelling wet food is better than all mild-smelling wet food. That said, some cats have their own peculiar tastes. These are some of the more unexpected foods cats tend to like—see if they're among your cat's favorites.

Homecooked turkey. (Not cat turkey, turkey roll, or turkey lunchmeat.) One friend of Ginger's, an otherwise silent cat, uttered the only meow of his entire life when faced with a Thanksgiving turkey that was not being sliced into the cat dish fast enough.

Tuna. A perennial favorite, but try other smelly seafood as well: mackerel, sardines, even shrimp. (Warning: If you happen to get any of these fresh, be sure to cook them before giving them to Fred—sashimi is not healthy for cats.)

Dried fishies in a bag. These are commonly available for a high price in pet stores, for a low price in Asian markets.

Popcorn. It's partly the salt, partly the cat-sized portability of the individual kernels. For even more enjoyment, pop popcorn in a pan without the lid on. Chasing all those flying kernels means frisky fun for Fred!

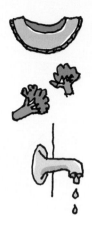

Cantaloupe. Who would guess that so many cats go gaga for a melon?

Cooked broccoli. True, it's not a fish, but it certainly can have a strong smell.

Water dribbling out of a faucet. Water isn't exactly a food, but cats are often attracted to running water more than to still water. It's moving, which is always attractive, and it's also fresh and aerated— what's not to like? You can also buy cat fountains that recirculate the water and thus provide a never-ending supply.

How to Make Special Kitty Treats

Make these for Fred and Ginger or for holiday packages to friends—just be sure to specify that, although humans could eat these, it's cats they're intended for!

In making and testing these treats, we assembled a panel of feline treat experts to comment on the palatability and deliciousness quotient of each. The panel of experts consisted of:

Fred: with an extensive background in canned catfood, Fred has been known to be choosy when it comes to cuisine outside the standard fare.

Ginger: a tuna aficionada, known for her finicky tastes.

Pouncer: striped, white-socked, lanky as a model, Pouncer is a happy-go-lucky treat enthusiast who never has to watch her weight.

Grizzle: darker-striped than Pouncer, Grizzle is a hardened veteran of the treat wars, interested but cautious around new food.

Mackerel Snackerels

These are like spoon-sized mackerel meatloaves.

WHAT YOU'LL NEED:

- ²/₃ cup (157 mL) canned mackerel
- ½ cup (118 mL) bread crumbs
- 1 tablespoon (15 mL) vegetable oil
- 1 egg, beaten

WHAT YOU'LL DO:

Preheat oven to 350° F (180° C). Combine the mackerel and the bread crumbs in a bowl and mix well. Add oil and egg and mix further. Drop snackerels onto a cookie sheet a spoonful at a time. Bake for 8 minutes. Cool before serving. Store leftover snackerels in the refrigerator.

OUR PANEL'S REACTIONS:

Fred: "I'm mildly interested. Not bad as an hors d'oeuvre. I'll eat some, but I think I'd like something meatier for the main course."

Ginger: "Well, it's not tuna. Frankly, mackerel isn't my favorite. Okay, I'll sniff it. It does smell intriguing. But no, too scary to taste. Sure you don't have any tuna?"

Pouncer: "It's not quite smelly enough for me, but I'll eat it to be polite."

Grizzle: "I'm dubious. Frankly, this looks like a congealed blob of glop."

FINAL SCORE: 2/4

Ginger's Sardine Delight

WHAT YOU'LL NEED:

- 1 can sardines, mashed into small pieces
- 1/3 cup (78 mL) cooked rice
- 1 tablespoon (15 mL) chicken liver, cooked
- 3 tablespoons (45 mL) parsley, chopped

WHAT YOU'LL DO:

Combine all ingredients. Requires no further cooking. Store in refrigerator.

Fred: "It looks like rice. But wait, it tastes like sardines!"

Ginger: "Well, this looks a bit suspicious. I definitely have not had this before, and furthermore it's not tuna. Okay, I'll sniff it. Okay, I'll taste it. Okay, I'll devour all of it. Is that all you're going to give me? It's named for me, after all! Doesn't that mean I get some more?"

Pouncer: "Oh, give me some of it, put it down here, oh, oh, do you have some more?"

Grizzle: "I will deign to overcome my reservations to sample a bit of this."

FINAL SCORE: 4/4

Down-Home Kitty Kornbread

WHAT YOU'LL NEED:

- ½ pound (220 g) chicken livers
- ¾ cup (177 mL) cornmeal
- 1 egg
- ¼ cup (60 mL) powdered milk
- 2 tablespoons (30 mL) unsulphured molasses

WHAT YOU'LL DO:

Preheat oven to 400° F (200° C). Put all ingredients into food processor and blend until they form a thick paste. Spread in baking pan. Bake for 10 minutes. Let cool and cut into bite-sized pieces. Store in refrigerator.

Fred: "This is an odd texture. Thank you for crumbling it for me. The bouquet is pleasing, but the actual taste is a bit peculiar. Don't you have some more of that sardine stuff?"

Ginger: "Okay, I'll sniff it. Maybe one nibble. Not bad."

Pouncer: "I'll eat this, but it's really a bit dense for my taste."

Grizzle: "Oh, for pete's sake. Where's the real cat food?"

FINAL SCORE: 2/4

Fishy Scramble

WHAT YOU'LL NEED:

- 1 egg
- 1 tablespoon (15 mL) cream
- 2 tablespoons (30 mL) tuna or mackerel
- small amount of butter

WHAT YOU'LL DO:

Whisk egg and cream together. Melt butter in frying pan and pour egg-cream mixture in. Stir to form scrambled eggs. When mixture is mostly cooked, add fish and stir further. Continue cooking for a few more moments until eggs are cooked through. Cool before serving. Break into pieces in cat dish.

Fred: "A delicate smelly fishiness—just what the master chef ordered."

Ginger: "Mmm, tuna. But what's this eggy business? I prefer my tuna neat."

Pouncer: "I should be pickier than this, but I've only had treats three times today, so I'll manage to stuff it down somehow."

Grizzle: "We are not amused."

FINAL SCORE: 2¹/2/4

Fred and Ginger also implore you to consult:

- Michele Bledsoe, *The Kitty Treats Cookbook* (2000)

- Kim Campbell Thornton and Jane Calloway, *Cat Treats* (1997)

- Carole Horstmeyer, *Gourmet Cat Treats: A Cookbook of Tasty Treats for Your Favorite Cat* (1997)

- Franki Papai Secunda, *The Cat Lover's Cookbook: Eighty-Five Fast, Economical, and Healthy Recipes for Your Cat* (1993)

- Rick Reynolds and Martha Reynolds, *Cat Nips! Feline Cuisine* (1993)

The Deluxe Kitty Birthday Party

A birthday is always a wonderful excuse for a party. If you don't know kitty's actual birthday, you can always choose a convenient day of the likely month, or just celebrate "Gotcha!" day, the day when kitty came to live with you. And as at any good birthday party, food, presents, and games are the order of the day. For kitty's birthday treat, choose one or more of kitty's favorite foods:

- ▶ catnip

- ▶ tuna

- ▶ turkey (fresh human-food turkey only; catfood turkey does not
  count as a Deluxe Treat)

- ▶ cooked, crumbled hamburger

- ▶ homemade kitty treats (see recipes on pages 86–90)

- ▶ your kitty's own particular beloved foods (you know what they are)

  Or you might try the Deluxe Kitty Birthday Steak Dinner!

Deluxe Kitty Birthday Steak Dinner

- about ²/₃ pound (300 g) filet mignon or sirloin steak
- bottle of good quality red wine

Cut steak in half. Broil one half, let cool somewhat, and mince finely or put through food grinder. Serve to delighted cat. Then broil other half, put on plate, apply sauce of your choice, open bottle of wine, spread tablecloth, and toast kitty's birthday while eating steak.

If you want to invite other humans to kitty's birthday party, of course, you might not want to invest in enough steak to feed everyone. You can order a cake with a cat on it from your local bakery or helpful grocery store. Or, if you're of a daring and unsqueamish constitution, you could present the assembled guests with the famous Cat Litterbox Cake.

Cat Litterbox Cake

WHAT YOU'LL NEED:

- 1 box chocolate cake mix
- 1 box white cake mix
- 1 package white sandwich cookies
- green food coloring
- 1 large package instant vanilla pudding
- 10 Tootsie rolls
- 1 small NEW cat litterbox, well washed
- 1 NEW cat-litter scooper, well washed

Prepare and bake cake mixes in any size pans. Prepare pudding. Pulverize cookies in blender in batches. Put one cup of pulverized cookies in bowl and mix with green food coloring; reserve the rest. When cakes have cooled, crumble them into a large bowl. Mix with half of the reserved white cookie crumbs and enough of the pudding to moisten the mixture. Pour mixture into clean litterbox. Take wrappers off Tootsie Rolls and heat in microwave until slightly soft. Bend and shape to resemble you-know-what (traditional contents of litterbox), then half-bury in cake mixture in litterbox. Sprinkle white cookie crumbs on top of cake mixture, then green cookie crumbs on top of white crumbs. Serve with cat-litter scooper to amazed or appalled guests.

It has to be said that this cake goes over better with children than with adults, and that it's often more an object of admiration than it is of consumption.

And what's a party without games? Fun games for cat lovers include:

▶ Group Kitty Haiku (see Chapter 3)

▶ The Kitty Instant Story-Maker (see Chapter 3)

▶ The First Eight Lives: What Great Person Has Been Reincarnated as Your Cat? (see Chapter 2)

Celebrate the occasion with presents for kitty. Time-tested gifts include:

▶ catnip, in pure or stuffed-mouse form (see Chapter 4)

▶ rhinestone or other fashionista collars (see Chapter 7)

▶ kitty furniture: scratching posts, beds, trees, tunnels, perches (see Chapter 4)

Or you could choose the most luxurious kitty gift of all: the Endless Lap Day. For those cats who want to be on a lap all the time, the Endless Lap Day is their big chance never to be pushed off just because the lap-owner has something better to do. The instructions are simple: when kitty gets on a lap, she gets to stay on the lap until she decides to get off. For lap-owners who've fortified themselves with trashy novels, snacks, and the remote control, the Endless Lap Day can have advantages even beyond making kitty happy. "Honey, isn't it your night to fix dinner? And Janie has strewn Legos all over the living room and Bernie overturned the bag of flour in the kitchen." Occupant of recliner gestures to kitty, curled up and snoring gently in lap: "Don't you remember? It's Ginger's Endless Lap Day—I can't get up till Ginger does. I'm afraid you'll have to take care of everything yourself. Sorry!" (Looks at Ginger fondly.)

Other Kitty Celebrations

Birthdays come around only once a year, and that's not nearly often enough for a celebration. When everyone is moping around the house and even wiggly string seems unenticing, try one of these:

Purrim

You may spell it Purim, but Fred and Ginger spell it Purrim because it's the most fun-loving and cat-happy of all Jewish holidays.

Purim, usually occurring in March, is the kind of celebration that makes Fred and Ginger most enthusiastic—because food is an important part. The traditional hamantaschen (tricornered cookies shaped like Haman's hat) are too fruity for cats, but triangular treats will fit the bill. You can, for instance, make tricornered Mackerel Snackerels (see page 86 for recipe). Fred calls them Mackereltaschen. And your cat would dearly love to be the recipient of a *mishloach manot*, the traditional gift basket of food (think cans of tuna, packets of treats, maybe a little lox?). That will certainly keep him occupied during the reading of the Megillah, even when the mention of Haman is disrupted by the traditional noisemakers. "Megillah!" says Fred. "He's that rough-looking tabby down the street. Talk about a noisemaker!"

St. Gertrude's Day (March 17)

St. Gertrude wasn't a cat herself, but she comes close to being an honorary feline. Born in the year 626 in what is now Belgium, she turned down marriage in favor of the holy life and became abbess of the monastery of Nivelles. Legend has it that she provides protection against mice and rats, and as recently as 1822 devotees left offerings of gold and silver mice at her shrine in Cologne. Pictures often show her with a cat sitting nearby. St. Gertrude was also regarded as a patron saint of gardeners, and good weather on March 17 meant spring planting could begin. She was, furthermore, a patron saint of travelers, and in particular protects against sea monsters; it was traditional to drink the "Sinte Geerts Minne" or "Gert-rudenminte" to the saint before setting out on a journey.

In honor of St. Gertrude, on March 17 your cat can be Gertude-for-a-Day. This will require an offering of a toy mouse (catnip might be better received than gold or silver!), and she should, of course, be treated with great veneration the whole day long. In recognition of St. Gertrude's role as patron saint of gardeners, plant a cat windowbox with catnip, cat thyme, or other cat-appealing flora (see Chapter 4). And to protect against those sea monsters, you'll want to indulge in the "Sinte Geerts Minne." For your cat, a dish of tuna juice is appropriate to the oceangoing theme. For yourself—well, if your cat could talk, she'd recommend the libation of your choice, would she not? Of course she would. Down the hatch!

A Midsummer Night's Dream

Midsummer Eve is the night when the fairy folk come out to dance, as Shakespeare knew well. Held on the summer solstice, it is still an important celebration in Scandinavia. (Does your cat like fish? That may well indicate a Scandinavian heritage—all the more reason to celebrate Midsummer Eve!) Why not have a Midsummer Eve party in which your cats can participate? Tradition calls for a bonfire (a campfire or even a candle will do) and walking the boundaries of your property (Fred will be glad to oblige). Dancing on the lawn is de rigueur, and Fred and Ginger can appear as the mischievous sprites they are. To make fairy halos, or cat tiaras, buy decorative strands spangled with stars at your

local craft store. Chenille stems or other pipe cleaners would also make elegant kitty headwear. Shape into a cat-sized halo and twine one end around Fred and Ginger's collars so that the halo hovers over their heads. They will hardly notice, but the halos will be a festive reminder of the night's celebration to everyone who sees them. Be sure to let Fred and Ginger celebrate with some nice Scandinavian fish (cooked).

First Snow-on-the-Paws Day

If you live in a snowy climate, this can be an annual treat. Fred's very first Snow-on-the-Paws Day is worthy of all-out celebration, of course, like a bar mitzvah or landmark birthday. You can also commemorate the occasion every year at the first snowfall. You might begin with a ritual reading from Robert Heinlein's novel *A Door into Summer*, which addresses the snow-outside-the-door situation. The most important part of the celebration, of course, is that Fred gets to go outside and walk in the snow. If you have a videocamera, a cat's first encounter with snow can be a prime comic moment (but don't laugh out loud! Fred's dignity must be preserved at all costs!). There may be much shaking of paws. If the snow is very deep, you can build snow Kitty Catstles or igloos for Fred's playtime. Thereafter, a nice warm bowl of snow-white cream is appropriate for Fred (and make some hot chocolate for yourself—Fred doesn't want you to feel left out on his big day).

Kitty Kristmas (December 25)

Ginger may not pay much heed to the origins of Christmas, but she'll certainly appreciate the abundance of dangly things! On the lower branches of the Christmas tree hang only things that are safe for her to bat at or chew on. Avoid tinsel—although it can sometimes go right through a cat, there are no guarantees, and it can be dangerous. Perhaps, instead, an ornamental mouse or bird? If Ginger's in an energetic frame of mind, she may just climb the entire tree, so it's best to Ginger-proof it with unbreakable ornaments.

Then, as Louisa May Alley-Cat said, "Christmas won't be Christmas without any presents"—so don't let this happen to poor Ginger. After all, Ginger's been good this year! It's easy to hang a kitty stocking from the mantel (see Chapter 4 on how to make a catnip sock). For the main present, Ginger points out that a nice cozy cat bed or a new toy wouldn't go amiss. And playing with the paper and the ribbon can be as much fun as the present itself.

Then there's the feasting. If turkey is your Christmas bird of choice, Ginger will be delighted; if you serve another kind of meat, give her a sniff to see if she wants a taste. (Like people, cats shouldn't overdo it at Christmas, tempting as indulgence is—be sure to encourage moderation.) "Fruitcake?" says Ginger. "Nasty! Don't get it near me!" Who said cats and humans were so different?

Boxing Day (December 26)

Although Boxing Day has been celebrated in Britain, Australia, New Zealand, and Canada for years, no one is sure exactly how it began. Perhaps the most plausible explanation is that it started as the day the wealthy boxed up goods to give to servants and the lower classes. Another theory is that alms boxes in churches were opened on that day, and the alms distributed to the poor. Fred and Ginger, however, maintain that the true origins of the holiday have been lost: it was originally intended to provide household cats with boxes to play in. "Reclaim the true spirit of Boxing Day!" says Ginger. Set out one box on the floor for your cat to play in. Nestle a blanket in another box, one with sides low enough so your cat can see out when lying down, and put the box in a high but cat-accessible place as a bed. With Boxing Day taken care of, Fred and Ginger may now lobby for the establishment of a Grocery Bagging Day.

Kitty Kwanzaa (December 26–January 1)

The seven days of Kwanzaa celebrate African culture and the strength of family and community—"and there is absolutely no reason," says Ginger, "to leave us out." Cats especially like quiet gatherings of people, as with the lighting of the candles each night of Kwanzaa. Your cat may appreciate the chance to sit on a lap and feel part of the gathering. Many families have developed individual rituals for each night of

Kwanzaa, and this is a chance to include Fred and Ginger as well—in readings, references to the family, photos, and, of course, in the feast on the sixth night of Kwanzaa. If the feast doesn't include a kitty-friendly food, give them a special dish of tuna or treats—and a special rub for being such a treasured member of the family.

Kitty Kalm

Although they're very accomplished at playing and eating, what cats are best at is relaxing—and no wonder, since they put in so much practice time! And the two best ways of relaxing are massage and catnapping. You can do both of these with Fred and Ginger. After all, when learning a skill, why not study with the experts?

Kitty Massage

Kitty massage has two variations: the one where you massage them, and the one where they massage you. The person-massages-cat variant is fairly simple, although both Fred and Ginger suggest that you practice it again and again until you get it right, and then keep your skills honed by putting in several hours a day of serious kitty-patting.

The rules for cat massage are simple: always stroke in the direction the fur grows, and don't press too hard. If Fred bites you or jumps down, you've pressed too hard.

Advanced kitty massagers know there are two strokes: the Full Hand Massage and the Butterfly Finger Variant. The Full Hand Massage speaks for itself: use your full hand. In the Butterfly Finger Variant, you move your thumb and index finger together and apart, gently, while your hand travels down kitty's spine, one finger on each side of the spine. Ooh—especially good near the tail! And if you do it right to a standing cat you will be rewarded by one of the most heartfelt cat responses: Elevator Butt.

For your massage expertise, here is a chart showing the places kitty most likes to be massaged. Note that cats, unlike dogs, generally do not like being stroked on top of their heads, and they especially do not like being patted there (which tends merely to

IMPORTANT KITTY MASSAGE POINTS
Massage areas are highlighted in blue

bounce their heads up and down and provoke unkind thoughts about the person doing the patting).

Then there is the variant where your kitty massages you. Begin with a sleepy cat with soft fur, preferably an old and agreeable sleepy cat with soft fur. Gently stroke your cheek against the cat's side. Or you can take off your shoes and socks and—again, very gently!—run your bare feet over the cat's back, as if stroking him with your feet. Feels as good to you as it does to him! As long as the cat holds still, you can give your arms a fur massage, or the backs of your hands, or your ankles. . . . You'll have to stop, though, as soon as the cat remembers he has claws. A chart of Important Human Massage Points is included for your information.

It is not recommended that you follow the example of a certain gentleman who shall remain nameless, who thought he could induce his cat to give him a back massage by rubbing hamburger on his bare back and coaxing the cat aboard. Don't even think of it! Pretend we never mentioned it! And remember, even declawed cats have claws on their back feet. Youch!

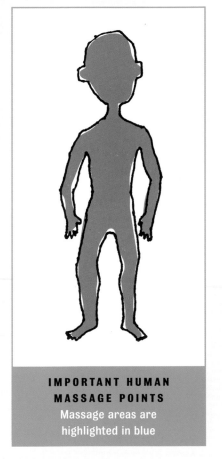

IMPORTANT HUMAN MASSAGE POINTS
Massage areas are highlighted in blue

Creative Catnapping

Solo Napping

Best on a lazy, warm afternoon. For cats, any sunny spot will do, even if the sun is artificially provided by means of a gooseneck lamp. Humans will prefer a shadier spot, ideally provided with a hammock. There are two positions: the Curl and the Stretch.

THE CURL

THE STRETCH

For optimum napping, these guidelines should be followed:

▶ Complete relaxation is a must.

▶ Loud noises, banging around the house, people starting up lawnmowers, cries of "Where is that Fred?" and all other extraneous distractions should be met only by a slight shift in position and a sinking into even deeper sleep.

▶ The only thing worth getting up for is dinner. Be sure to stretch and yawn a lot.

Cat/Cat Napping

The most cosmically advanced cat/cat napping position is, of course, the Yin/Yang—even better if the cats in question are black and white!

More advanced cats may try the cat/cat/cat/cat napping position, something that comes naturally to kittens.

Cat/Human Napping

Two species doing what they each do so well—what would be more artistic? Favored arrangements include:

Yin/Big Yang

(like the Yin/Yang, only the Yang is a lot larger than the Yin)

Cat Necktie

(well, cats do like to lie on your chest)

The Double Stretch

(and its variant, the Stretch-in-Arms)

Undercover Agent

(we get under the covers— why shouldn't they?)

Kitty Kare

Keeping Fred and Ginger safe and healthy is important—and it needn't be all work and no play. Since cats will never do anything unless it's worth doing, kitty exercise should be enjoyable as well as invigorating, and the same goes for kitty nutrition and even kitty safety. From the Treat-at-the-Top-of-the-Stairs maneuver to kosmic kitty krystals, attention to kitty kare will help you enjoy many long years of kitty kapers together.

Kitty Exercise

When most of your day is spent relaxing in the sun, the weight does tend to creep on—as Ginger can testify. Overweight cats are subject to many of the same ills as hefty humans, so you'll want to give Ginger plenty of opportunities to stay in fighting trim. And as we all know, making exercise fun is key. Fortunately, there are a number of fun ways to give Ginger a workout—and to give yourself some exercise at the same time.

Fishing for Fred

Health experts have long advised adding fish to the diet. When you make a kitty fishing rod toy, Fred can follow this admonition as well.

WHAT YOU'LL NEED:

- a fishing rod 4–5 feet (1.2–1.5 m) long, or any flexible pole or stick of a similar length
- 3 feet (1 m) thin stretchable cord (often used to wrap gifts)
- duct tape
- cat toy or crinkled cellophane
- needle and thread (optional)

WHAT YOU'LL DO:

Tie the stretchable cord to one end of the pole, and wrap duct tape neatly around the knot so the cord won't come off. On the other end of the cord, tie the fish by its tail. If you want to assure that the fish will never come off, you can also sew the fish to the cord, just where the back fin would be. If you're using another cat toy, tie or sew it on the cord as appropriate, or you could just tie on a wad of crinkled cellophane. Then go fishing for Fred. Bob the fish up and down in front of him. Soon he should be batting at the fish, then leaping after it. Let him catch it from time to time, and pull the cord tight; the stretchiness of the cord will bounce the fish away from him when he lets his grip slip.

You can fish for Fred while lazing in the recliner, but for more exercise for both of you, trail the cord around the room, making the fish slither after you. With the running, leaping, and grabbing this kind of fishing inspires, this is one of the most athletic pastimes Fred can enjoy.

Treat-at-the-Top-of-the-Stairs

Some cats are too out of shape to start with vigorous exercise. For them, there's the Treat-at-the-Top-of-the-Stairs maneuver.

WHAT YOU'LL NEED:

- a house with stairs
- your cat's dinner

With Ginger at the bottom of the stairs, simply serve Ginger's dinner at the top of the stairs, so she has to climb up them to get dinner. It's more fun to exercise when there's a treat at the end, isn't it? For greater solidarity with Ginger, give yourself a treat at the top of the stairs, too—but set a good example by making it something healthy!

The Two-Cat Perpetual Workout

The most reliable way to make sure your cat exercises is to get a second cat, the source of an almost perpetual workout. If your cat is a sedate, set-in-her-ways older cat, another adult cat may put her nose out of joint, but a new kitten may be just the ticket. Keep the kitten in a separate room for a few days while you let them sniff each other through the door, and supervise their first meetings. Soon the irresistible bounciness of the kitten will get your cat moving—even if it is away from the small sprite trying to chew on her tail!

More likely, though, they will be chasing each other down the hallway, through the living room, up and over the sofa . . . and they'll both be getting plenty of exercise. You'll get exercise, too, as you spring up to check on the latest crash in the next room.

Kitty Nutrition

Commercial catfoods provide a well-balanced diet, but there's also the element of fun to consider. Kitty favorite plants and treats (described in chapters 4 and 5) help spice up life. But you can take your quest for good health and good fun one further by growing wheatgrass—a treat for Fred, a fun project for you, and a nutritional supplement for you both. Cats love to munch on the grass, and it's said to aid kitty digestion. What's more, many people swear by wheatgrass juice as a nutritional pick-me-up. One warning: although Fred will like munching on the grass, it's less tasty to humans—growing it may be more fun than drinking it!

Wheatgrass (For Cats)

WHAT YOU'LL NEED:

- a seed tray (available in garden stores)
- enough peat moss to fill half the seed tray, plus a little extra
- enough potting soil to fill half the seed tray
- wheat berries. These small hard berries can be bought at health food stores— be sure the store has a high turnover, or the berries may be too old to sprout. Buy enough to fill your seed tray when densely scattered.
- a sunny windowsill

111

1. Rinse the berries, then put them in a bowl with enough water to immerse them. Cover with a dishtowel or cheesecloth. Let sit 12 hours.

2. Drain the water but let the seeds remain damp, covering them with a damp paper towel.

3. Let sit a further 12 hours, rinsing them and re-covering once during this period. When you remove the paper towel at the end of this period, you will see sprouts beginning to appear.

4. Fill the seed tray with a 50/50 mixture of peat moss and potting soil. Spread the berries on the soil in a single layer, making sure the berries don't overlap. Sprinkle the extra peat moss over the berries in a single thin layer.

5. Water the tray to moisten. Do not overwater or the berries will develop mold.

6. Put in a sunny window and water as needed to keep soil moist, being careful not to overwater. If plants droop, change to a window with partial shade.

Wheatgrass grows quite fast, and should be ready for Fred to nibble in as little as four to seven days.

Fred likes his wheatgrass still in the seed tray and will nibble it happily as long as it thrives. Wheatgrass requires a little more preparation for human consumption.

Wheatgrass Juice (For Humans)

WHAT YOU'LL NEED:

- all materials for growing wheatgrass (as above)
- a juicer
- a glass
- an intrepid constitution

WHAT YOU'LL DO:

Grow wheatgrass as described above. When it is around seven inches (18 cm) high, snip off an ounce (28 g) of the grass and juice it in the juicer. Pour the thick green juice into a glass and hold your nose—down the hatch! Gives you new respect for cows, doesn't it? For added palatability, mix the ounce of wheatgrass juice with three times the amount of carrot juice. Experts recommend starting with a single ounce of wheatgrass juice and, if desired, working up gradually to four ounces per day.

After you've snipped off the tops, the grass will grow back, but the second growth is said to be less nutritious. This won't bother Fred—he'll be happy to nibble until the cows come home.

Other Healthy Treats

Unlikely as it may seem, many cats just adore furball medicine (the kind that looks like a gel and comes in a tube, sold under a number of brand names). This is perhaps because one of the chief ingredients is cod-liver oil. For cats with furballs, most kinds can be taken daily, and the manufacturer recommends two to three dabs a week for furball prevention.

"Love the stuff!" says Fred. "This is fun for me—but is giving me a dab once a day fun for the Big Guy?" Yes—not cleaning furballs off the carpet is always fun.

Kitty Safety

Keeping your cat healthy is just one part of taking care of him—safety is equally important! Make sure you know how to protect your kitty from the perils in the world.

Going Outdoors

Does your cat go outdoors? It's a sad fact that, according to estimates, the lifespan of indoor cats is twice that of outdoor cats. Cats who go outdoors are subject to diseases, toxic plants and other substances, attacks from dogs, other cats, and wild animals, and, most hazardous of all, the danger of cars.

It has to be said that cats do love being outdoors, however, even if all they have the chance to do is chew on a little grass and sniff the air. Fortunately, there are several compromises available: ways your cat can experience the fun of the outdoors and stay safe as well. You might consider one of these possibilities.

An outdoor catspace. Folks who are both ambitious and handy with tools can build special outdoor cat enclosures, sometimes accessed via catdoors. If you choose to make a catspace, remember that your enclosure needs a roof (best, since it will protect against rain), or at the very least catproof netting over the top, or many cats will work out how to go "over the wall." Prebuilt cat enclosures somewhat like aviaries are also advertised in the back of many cat magazines. For extra kitty satisfaction, install shelves at different heights, for your cat to lie on, and perhaps even a climbable tree trunk or two. "And if it's like an aviary," says Ginger, "does that mean you'll put a bird in?" This may be cat safety, but putting a bird in would definitely not be bird safety.

A catproof yard. Another option is a securely fenced yard. For the fence to be truly secure, there should be no trees that might provide access, and the fence must be quite high with no footholds or intermediate stages. Your cat's fitness will determine how high the fence needs to be: an old and creaky cat may not be able to manage much height at all, whereas a cat in fine fettle might easily manage a high fence in a single bound. It goes without saying that cats should not be able to fit between the slats of the fence. For those with a yard that can be fenced adequately, this makes an ideal cat playground. You can add special kitty amusements as well, such as peepholes through the fence at cat's-eye level, or a kitty-house with a roof flat enough for cat sunbathing.

Cat supervision. The simplest method of all may be simply to go outside with your cat. Take your seat in a lawn chair or laze in a hammock with a novel: these pursuits are entirely justified if you label them "Fred's exercise time." Or you can just keep an eye out the back door. The best time for Fred's exercise is just before mealtime. Fred gets a five- or ten-minute romp in the grass, and then the sound of the can opener is heard through the open door—chances are he'll be back in a flash.

Lost and Found

If Ginger goes astray, you want her to be able to sing the line from "Amazing Grace": "I once was lost, but now I'm found." The best way to assure this is with an ID tag, and of course the ID tag has to go on a collar worthy of Ginger's acute fashion sense. Begin with a plain collar, ideally a breakaway collar, which will pull apart if snagged on something. Breakaway collars are usually made of a stretchy material other than leather, which also makes them easier to decorate. Just add one or more of the following:

- **reflective tape** (red or yellow, or both, wrapped around the collar in stripes)

- **sequins** (sew them on with a heavy needle)

- **rhinestones** (craft stores sell devices, like modified staple guns, which will attach rhinestones)

- **a small crystal** (use the kind that hangs from a necklace, and hang it from Ginger's collar on a light ring of the type that the ID tag is attached to; be sure it's not too heavy! Then Ginger can be a kosmic kitty.)

- **a charm** (use a charm from your charm bracelet—a cat, a mouse, a four-leaf clover? Just make sure it's not a design that can get snagged on anything. "Entirely suitable," says Ginger, "because I have natural charm.")

- **a tag** (write out Ginger's name, phone number, and address on a small piece of card stock; laminate it using clear packing tape, and attach it with a small metal ring)

Other Kitty Necessities

The necessities of life go beyond food and shelter, as Fred and Ginger will testify. They also include:

Warmth. Especially important to cats! Put a soft blanket on a high surface, point a gooseneck lamp down at the blanket, and you have Fred heaven. If the sun hits certain areas of the floor at certain times of day, put a blanket or catbed down on those areas, and you know where you'll find Fred. You can also get pads of non-toxic gel, which can be heated in the microwave, and slip them under Fred's blanket. Pure cat bliss! Now might be the time to get out the camera . . .

Routine. Cats dote on predictability. Produce breakfast at the same time every morning, and rearrange the furniture at your peril! They like to know they can count on a lap every Tuesday when you sit down for your favorite TV show. And they especially like the predictability of treats—preferably at least once a day. If you serve a treat at the same time every day, Fred and Ginger have the fun of looking forward to it, and you have the relief of not being pestered until treat time is near. Well, not much, anyway.

Variety. Then again, the same old toys can get a bit wearisome, and the catnip smell goes out of them after a while. Why not a new toy, a new flavor of treat (providing it's a good flavor, of course), and some fresh catnip scent on the scratching post?

Sociability. "I am not aloof," says Ginger. "That's slander! What I am is choosy." But even the choosiest cat can crave company, even if she sits at a distance of six feet with her back turned. Greet your cat when she meets you at the door. Waggle your eyebrows at her as she looks up at you from that sunny spot. Give her a nice

luxurious brushing as you watch *Born Free* together. When you're about to change the sheets, let her know, and take an extra minute in the Changing-the-Sheets Game. You don't need a big block of time to remind her that she's a valuable member of the household and that, no matter how busy you are at the moment, soon you'll be kapering together again.

Quick Cat Health Reference Guide

(photocopy so you have one for each of your cats)

Cat's name _____

Approximate date of birth _____

Special identifying features _____

_____

_____

Last vaccinations _____

_____

_____

Chronic health conditions _____

_____

Treatment for chronic health conditions _____

_____

Cat-sitter's name and number _____

Veterinarian's name _____

Veterinarian's phone number _____

Name and address of 24-hour or emergency vet _____

_____

_____

Number of 24-hour or emergency vet _____

ASPCA National Animal Poison Control Center: 1 (888) 426-4435
(Accessible from the U.S. only; have your credit card ready)

Camuti Memorial Feline Consultation and Diagnostic Service:
1 (800) KITTY-DR (1 (800) 548-8937)
(Accessible from the U.S. only; have your credit card ready)
Veterinarians available by phone 9 A.M.–noon and 2–4 P.M., U.S. Eastern time on Mondays,
Wednesdays, and Fridays, excluding holidays. Overview available at
www.vet.cornell.edu/Public/FHC/camuti.html.

Resources on the Web

Big Game Playing

Ideas for outdoor cat entertainment

www.corporatevideo.com/klips/catfun.htm

Kitty Characteristics

Cat astrology

www.skittlescam.com/fun/astrology/index.html

Kitty Kulture

Video Catnip, Cat TV, The Adventures
of Betty Bird, The Adventures of
Freddy Fish, The Adventures of Larry
Lizard, The Adventures of Krazy Kats
Available from Pet A Vision,

www.cattv.com/VideosforCats.htm

Kitty show video toy

http://videoforcats.com

CyberPounce

www.CyberPounce.com

Catsbuzz

http://members.aol.com/catsbuzz

Kitty Krafts

Do-it-yourself cat tree

http://amby.com/cat_site/cattree.html

Cat climber

http://members.home.net/david-
rebecca/Catclimber.html

Make-it-yourself cat window perch

www.diynet.com/DIY/article/0,2058,2726,FF.html

Kooking for Kitty

Recipes for your cat

www.recipesource.com/misc/pet-food/cat

www.catscans.com/recipes.htm

Kitty Kalm

Kitty massage
http://messybeast.com/catmassage.htm
http://home.talkcity.com/PramPlaza/
    dodad-cl/massage.html

Kitty Kare

Feline first aid
www.sniksnak.com/cathealth/firstaid.html

Plants poisonous to cats
www.cfainc.org/articles/plants.html

Cat health resources
(from Cornell University College
of Veterinary Medicine)
http://web.vet.cornell.edu/Public/FHC/
    FelineHealth.html

Suggestions for dealing with stray and feral cats
(from Alley Cat Allies)
www.alleycat.org

Cats in General

The Original Cat Ring
www.xmission.com/~emailbox/catring.html

Index and links to cat sites
http://dir.yahoo.com/Science/Biology/Zoology/
    Animals_Insects_and_Pets/Mammals/Cats